Praise for *Fear Gone Wild*

"Kayla is a good friend of mine. She has a message for us not about loss, but about being real. Filled with honesty and vulnerability, Kayla doesn't just inform us about mental health, love, and loss; she invites us to actively participate in lives filled with greater purpose, authenticity, and awareness."

—BOB GOFF, AUTHOR OF *NEW YORK TIMES* BESTSELLERS
LOVE DOES AND *EVERYBODY, ALWAYS*

"*Fear Gone Wild* pulls back the curtain that shrouds mental illness in the church. With tempered strength and well-chosen words, my friend Kayla gently moves aside the heavy fabric so that we might see the pain up close and learn alongside her. This book transforms the beautiful love story of Andrew and Kayla into a vehicle of hope and rescue for others. I cried as I read her words, yet found myself strangely encouraged that their loss could mean restoration for countless others."

—LISA BEVERE, *NEW YORK TIMES* BESTSELLING AUTHOR

"*Fear Gone Wild* is courageous and honest; a timely message for all of us today. Kayla's story of navigating through Andrew's death, and learning about the mental illness he walked through, is written with tenderness, bravery, and hope. Her heart and soul cover these pages with a passion to help us better understand mental illness and to have hope that God is with us every step of the way. We highly recommend getting a copy of this book!"

—CHAD AND JULIA VEACH, LEAD PASTORS OF ZOE CHURCH, LOS ANGELES

"I cried while reading *Fear Gone Wild*. I cried not only for the devastation and sorrow Kayla and her family have experienced, but also because I recognize so much of my family's sorrow in hers. We've both lost someone we dearly loved to suicide and share the crushing shock, horror, and pain that accompany such a death. But we also share the same rock-solid hope that God is at work in the losses; walking with us, carrying us when needed, gently reminding that he will never abandon us in our grief and is in the process of restoring the ruins of our lives. Kayla's beautiful way with words will comfort your aching heart."

—KAY WARREN, COFOUNDER OF SADDLEBACK CHURCH

"Absolutely powerful! Wow! I was so deeply moved by Kayla's words and story. *Fear Gone Wild* is filled with epic truth, wisdom, and practical insights that will forever change you and the way you see the struggle for mental health. This book is a precious gift to us all."

—MIKE FOSTER, AUTHOR AND EXECUTIVE COUNSELOR

"When Kayla Stoecklein speaks we all lean in. Her gentle strength is a force and her honest faith speaks to the most tender, hidden parts of the soul. She has chosen, right in the middle of her own personal grief, to walk openly through her unimaginable pain so that others around the world can find hope in the middle of their own tragedies. Her story has challenged the church at large to take a closer, more compassionate and educated look at the impact of mental illness and the reality of spiritual warfare. Andrew's legacy is one of a man of faith who lived to serve others. As you read *Fear Gone Wild*, Kayla reveals that there is hope, even through the deepest loss, because of the God we serve."

—DAWNCHERÉ WILKERSON, PASTOR OF VOUS CHURCH, MIAMI

"As a longtime mental health professional and fierce advocate, this book hits home and strikes a vital chord. The pain and power poetically shared through her raw truth and courage are so needed in the world today. Thank you, Kayla, for honoring your loss and using your story, wisdom, and heart in such a poignant and compelling way."

—MILES ADCOX, OWNER AND CEO OF ONSITE TENNESSEE

FEAR GONE WILD

FEAR GONE WILD

A STORY OF MENTAL ILLNESS, SUICIDE, AND HOPE THROUGH LOSS

KAYLA STOECKLEIN

NELSON
BOOKS
An Imprint of Thomas Nelson

Published in Nashville, Tennessee, by Nelson Books, an imprint of Thomas Nelson. Nelson Books and Thomas Nelson are registered trademarks of HarperCollins Christian Publishing, Inc.

Author is represented by The Fedd Agency, Inc., P. O. Box 341973, Austin, Texas 78734.

Thomas Nelson titles may be purchased in bulk for educational, business, fundraising, or sales promotional use. For information, please email SpecialMarkets@ThomasNelson.com.

Unless otherwise noted, Scripture quotations taken from The Holy Bible, New International Version®, NIV®. Copyright © 1973, 1978, 1984, 2011 by Biblica, Inc.® Used by permission of Zondervan. All rights reserved worldwide. www.Zondervan.com. The "NIV" and "New International Version" are trademarks registered in the United States Patent and Trademark Office by Biblica, Inc.®

Scripture quotations marked ESV are taken from the ESV® Bible (The Holy Bible, English Standard Version®). Copyright © 2001 by Crossway, a publishing ministry of Good News Publishers. Used by permission. All rights reserved.

Scripture quotations marked KJV are taken from the King James Version. Public domain.

Scripture quotations marked THE MESSAGE are taken from The Message. Copyright © 1993, 2002, 2018 by Eugene H. Peterson. Used by permission of NavPress. All rights reserved. Represented by Tyndale House Publishers, Inc.

Scripture quotations marked NLT are taken from the Holy Bible, New Living Translation. © 1996, 2004, 2015 by Tyndale House Foundation. Used by permission of Tyndale House Publishers, Inc., Carol Stream, Illinois 60188. All rights reserved.

Scripture quotations marked TPT are from The Passion Translation®. Copyright © 2017, 2018 by Passion & Fire Ministries, Inc. Used by permission. All rights reserved. ThePassionTranslation.com.

Scripture quotations marked THE VOICE are taken from The Voice™. © 2012 by Ecclesia Bible Society. Used by permission. All rights reserved. Note: Italics in quotations from The Voice are used to "indicate words not directly tied to the dynamic translation of the original language" but that "bring out the nuance of the original, assist in completing ideas, and . . . provide readers with information that would have been obvious to the original audience" (The Voice, preface).

Any internet addresses, phone numbers, or company or product information printed in this book are offered as a resource and are not intended in any way to be or to imply an endorsement by Thomas Nelson, nor does Thomas Nelson vouch for the existence, content, or services of these sites, phone numbers, companies, or products beyond the life of this book.

ISBN 978-1-4002-1768-7 (eBook)
ISBN 978-1-4002-1767-0 (HC)

Library of Congress Control Number: 2020939916

Printed in the United States of America

20 21 22 23 24 LSC 10 9 8 7 6 5 4 3 2 1

To my Andrew,
May your life always be defined by the way
you lived, not the way you died.
This is just a small part of your story.
Love you forever,
Your girl

Contents

Foreword

by Lysa TerKeurst

This is a message of *both/and*. It's crucial we approach this message as both a love story full of life and a tragedy full of loss at the same time. When we leave room for both/and in another person's story, we start to leave space in our own life for both sorrow and celebration to coexist.

As Kayla brings her story, her heart, her tears, her brokenness, and her healing to these pages, I pray you and I bring something too. I pray we bring our willingness to enter this tender place with enough humility to admit we need this message and enough humanity to set aside all harsh opinions. The both/and of this story is that it's one of both darkness and victory. It's both wondrous and will leave you wondering why. It's both comforting and tragic. It's both full of answers and questions. It's both full of brilliance and bottoming out. It's both a breathtaking love story and a breath stealing gut punch.

Andrew was both a captivating speaker, loving pastor, invested father, and smitten husband, and a man haunted by a darkness that wrestled him to the ground. We must let the enormous light and love of Andrew stay as authentic as it truly was, without rewriting his death by suicide or rescripting any piece of his beautiful legacy. We don't deny any part of his mental illness; that's part of this story for sure. But it's only a part. We are all carriers of sorrow, struggle, and burdens that are hidden in the shadows, still chasing us from hard yesterdays. Through my conversations and processing with Kayla, I've learned a few things I need to know to be a better friend, a better mom, and a more equipped human in our world full of people fighting to win their own battles with mental illness. And I've learned to be kinder to myself.

This book isn't one you'll be able to read and put on a shelf. It's one that will move into your soul and stay there a long, long while. And oh, what a welcomed treasure these words will be. I knew from the first blog post of Kayla's I read that she was destined to get this book out into the wild. No message like the one pouring out from her heart should stay caged.

We are unfinished, but my beautiful, brave, bold friend Kayla will help us all know we are not unseen. This book was always meant to make its way to you and me. Now, bring your heart out from hiding. There's nothing to fear. There's nothing to shrink back from. Your tenderness and your toughness are both welcome here. I'm going to take your hand and place it in Kayla's and let her take you on this journey. I am safe with her and so are you.

Now, let's turn this page and trust the wise words Andrew constantly proclaimed, "God's got this." Indeed, he does.

—Lysa TerKeurst

ONE

The Story Before
the Story

It wasn't always wild. No, my life was actually quite predictable—and good. *Very* good.

I had it all. The man, the kids, the beautiful home, and even the mom car. My future was full of vibrant colors, grand adventures, and wonderful purpose—until it wasn't. When fear crept into our home, it dimmed the lights and swiftly spread like wildfire. Our peaceful home, our predictable life, our hopeful future, all set ablaze by mental illness.

I wish I could say our story is unique, but it isn't. The reality is, all across the world, beautiful families like ours are engulfed by the flames of mental illness. In the US alone, one in five adults (47.6 million people) will experience mental illness in a given year.[1]

The mind is complex, which makes treating mental illness complicated. I'll never forget hearing these words from a seasoned psychiatrist: "We know but a drop in the ocean about the brain." One single drop, in a vast open sea. There is still a long way to go and incredible work to be done to understand the human mind.

I'll be the first to admit I haven't always sought to understand or empathize with those suffering from the debilitating effects of mental illness. In the past, I've been guilty of ignoring its existence—diminishing it as a whim or an exaggeration perpetuated by the person suffering. But now I know better. Now I see mental illness from a new perspective, and my once hardened heart is full of compassion and empathy.

I had a front-row seat to the paralyzing and devastating impact that mental illness has on "ordinary people"—even the most faithful of Christians—and the excruciating damage it can leave in its wake. When my husband, Andrew, the man of my dreams and my heart, received his diagnosis, I was forced to reckon with the very present and powerful reality of mental illness in a new way.

Before I share our intricate journey, though, I feel compelled to first share with you our story before the sad story. The love story that began our relationship. We lived a big life in our short time together and experienced trials and hardships most people don't face in their early twenties. We were on the fast track from the day we met—a day I'll never forget.

Andrew lived on the second floor of a weathered house that was situated directly on the sand overlooking the beautiful blue Pacific Ocean in Newport Beach, California. The house was home to a group of young men affectionately known throughout our college campus (Vanguard University) as "the beach-house guys." I knew all about the infamous guys because one of my best friends was dating one of them. During one visit to the beach house, she jokingly pulled out a picture of herself and her friends to show these curious guys. Andrew's eyes scanned the photo, and he pointed at me. "Her," he said.

A few days later, with a stomach full of butterflies and my friend by my side (I was too afraid to go alone), I walked down the small alleyway and up the narrow staircase to meet a guy who had picked me out of a photo. As we opened the door and walked inside, my heart and mind raced.

I wasn't the girl guys typically picked out of pictures. I was clumsy and awkward, shy and insecure. In high school I made my own clothes from articles picked up at the local thrift store, wore men's neckties in my hair because I thought it looked "cool," and hid behind thick bangs that swooped over the side of my face, covering my left eye completely. To top it all off, I proudly told anyone who asked about my future, "I never want to get married, and I never want to have kids." I was the last person anyone thought would be wearing a "ring by spring," but that was before I met Andrew.

When I walked through the door, my eyes met his, and my heart leaped. He was tall, thin, and handsome—a well-dressed guy, wearing an oversized flannel shirt, dark skinny jeans, and sandals. I swooned over his deep blue eyes, neatly combed brown hair, and quiet confidence. He wasn't the loudest one in the room, but his presence was magnetic.

We spent the evening with a couple of friends, riding fixed-gear bikes to the pier. I knew right away Andrew was athletic. He hopped on the bike and took off like a pro. And me, well, the bike I was borrowing was too tall, so my feet couldn't reach the ground. Once I finally got the bike to move, I wasn't quite sure how to stop because, as I quickly realized, fixed-gear bikes don't have brakes. As we made our way in the dark to the pier, I weaved all over the road, ran into a fire hydrant, and even grazed a parked car. By the time we made it back to the beach house, I was convinced there was no way this guy was going to fall for me, the clumsy, shy girl with bangs who could hardly ride a bike.

I'm so glad I was wrong.

A few days later he sent me a message on Facebook asking for my phone number, and the following week, he picked me up for our first date—no bikes, no friends, just the two of us. It was November 4, 2008, the day Barack Obama won the election to become president of the United States, which we found out from our waitress midway through dinner. We sat at a small wooden table in a dimly lit coffeehouse. I sipped on a chai tea latte while he worked his way through a salad, and we slowly began to unravel the mystery of each other.

I learned he was the oldest of three. He had a brother and a sister, and his parents pastored Inland Hills Church, a local church they'd founded about forty minutes from our college campus in a city called Chino. He'd gone to college hoping to step away from ministry and into a career in communications, but midway through his sophomore year, he realized he was made for ministry. Now a junior, he had just been offered a position as the junior-high director at Inland Hills Church. As a girl who loved God and grew up highly involved in church, I thought I'd hit the jackpot. Andrew loved God, he was undeniably attractive, he came from a solid family, and he was driven to succeed. My story was much different.

I came from a broken home and was still recovering from my parent's abrupt divorce a few years prior. He listened as I shared how lost I felt in my family, in my pain, and in my life. I didn't know who I was, and I hadn't yet figured out who I wanted to become. I had already switched my college major three times and still felt unsure about where I'd land. But none of that seemed to faze him. His big blue eyes pierced through my complicated mess and saw my potential. He was full of grace and empathy, and by the end of the night, he asked me out again. For our third date we went to a Coldplay concert, and afterward we kissed in the rain. Ours was a fast fall into love.

There were a million reasons why I was attracted to Andrew, but one of the biggest was he knew where he was going. Andrew was good at anything he tried. I knew no matter what he did in life, he would be successful. After growing up in a home of uncertainty, I sought Andrew as my safe place. I believed life with him would be beautiful and certain. I knew together we could build a life I'd be proud to call ours. I was no longer the shy, awkward girl who didn't want to get married; instead I found myself, less than a year after we met, hand in hand with the man of my dreams, shopping for a wedding ring.

During a girls' weekend away in San Diego, Andrew surprised me at a small park on Coronado Island when he jumped out of the bushes, covered my eyes with his cold hands, walked me down to the water, and—in front of all of my closest girlfriends—got down on one knee and asked me to be his wife. The following year, on December 10, 2010, I married the man of my dreams.

Like many lovestruck newlyweds, we wanted to blaze our own trail as a couple. So when Andrew was offered a position as the high school pastor at a small church surrounded by thick green trees in the suburbs of rainy Seattle, we jumped at the opportunity. During our days in the Northwest, we leaned into God and each other as we figured out how to be married far away from home. We were surprised when, only six months later, we felt a stirring in our hearts calling us back to sunny Southern California and to Inland Hills, where Andrew accepted a new position as the creative arts director.

Less than four months later, we understood why the move had been necessary: in the fall of 2011, Andrew's father, Dave, was diagnosed with aggressive acute lymphoblastic leukemia. The devastating news rocked our family and stunned our church. Andrew was thrust from his role as the creative arts director into a position of leadership alongside his dad, his best friend, who was fighting hard for his life. At only twenty-three years old, Andrew was in many ways standing in as lead pastor over the church. He was behind the scenes, planning messages, booking guest speakers, and organizing staff meetings—as well as speaking regularly from the stage on Sundays.

In May 2015, as Dave's health continued to decline, Andrew received the official baton to carry our church into the future as the lead pastor. It was monumental for our family and church. Dave, who had been bound to a wheelchair due to spinal cord damage caused by chemotherapy, was wheeled onto the stage for the announcement, and we all surrounded Andrew with love and support. I beamed with pride and gazed in awe at my Andrew, my husband, the guy who I fully believed could withstand the pressure and rise to the challenge set before him. During the four-year leukemia journey, Andrew and I welcomed two boys to our family—Smith and Jethro. Dave passed away in October 2015 due to a final relapse, and six months later, we added our third boy, Brave, in April 2016.

Andrew loved me and his boys deeply. He often spent his days off working on projects around the house. The ultimate handyman, he figured out how to change the switches in the bathroom to automatically turn on when we walked into the room; he shiplapped our entire entryway, put a sprinkler system in the front yard, and even installed laminate flooring all throughout our first home. If I wanted my house to look like one of Chip and Joanna Gaines's, he would make it happen. I was incredibly proud of my man, and I was bold about sharing my feelings of pride and praise with others.

I want you to know my Andrew for who he was. This is the man I fell madly in love with. This is the healthy Andrew I wanted to grow old with, the man I chose to live out my forever with. When his mind was fit and strong, he would have never predicted his life would come to a sudden and tragic end by suicide at only thirty years old.

But it did. Mental illness came rushing into our world at full speed, and before we could even catch our breath, he was gone. How did we go from living our dream life to living our worst nightmare? There is so much I would do differently if I could do it all over again, and if Andrew were here, I'm confident he would do the same.

I've come to hate parts of the story I share in these pages. I would have never chosen them. Maybe you, too, are living in a reality you never saw coming. If you are walking alongside someone who is struggling with mental illness, then the words in this book are for you. If you are facing a mental health diagnosis you never saw coming, then the words in this book are for you. If you've lost someone you loved to suicide, then the words in this book are for you. If you have never been touched by the pain of mental illness and know absolutely nothing about it, then the words in this book are still for you. Why? Because we all need to hear this message. We all need to be better equipped and educated when it comes to mental health.

Today, *right now*, this moment matters. I believe God wants to meet us right where we are. In this book you may not find all of the answers you are looking for, but you will find a friend who understands your pain and an even greater Friend who calls you by name. One way or another, we will find our way again as we journey through the unexpected wilderness—not alone, but together.

TWO

The Uninvited Guest

I could hear him pacing back and forth, back and forth. I opened my eyes just enough to see what was going on. I was tired. Motherhood was wearing on me, grinding my whole body into exhaustion every single day. Yet I sensed he needed me too, this dark, tall, nervous shadow at the end of our bed, wearing old worn slippers on his feet, a brown robe draped over his thin frame, thick hair in disarray. He needed me, and I loved him, and love, sometimes inconvenient, woke me up in the middle of the night.

"Babe, what's going on?" I muttered in a raspy voice. "What are you doing awake? Why are you walking around?" He continued pacing.

"My chest," he whispered. "My chest is burning. It's so tight, I can't breathe."

"Do I need to call somebody? Do I need to take you somewhere?" Still drowsy and terribly confused, I wondered if this was all a dream.

"No," he answered. "I'll be okay. I think I might be having a panic attack."

I sat up. "A panic attack? What do you mean you think you might be having a panic attack?" He kept his pace, back and forth, back and forth, not too fast, not too slow, focused and determined.

I had grown used to his tossing and turning. Andrew hardly ever had a peaceful night of sleep. I would often wake up in the middle of the night to him watching TV or working on his computer, but this was different.

Rambling on, I questioned, "Since when do you have panic attacks? Do you even know what a panic attack is? When did this start happening? What are you afraid of? Why can't you relax?" I wasn't thinking clearly. In my exhaustion I just wanted him to stop being "so dramatic" and lie back down. I offered to rub his back or run a bath for him, but my solutions weren't working. He wasn't stopping. He began to pace faster, more determined, growing angry.

"Andrew, why are you ignoring me? I'm trying to help you." I spoke louder now, wide awake.

"You don't understand. I can't get it to stop." His voice was stern. "I've been up for hours. I haven't slept at all. It just keeps getting worse." He continued pacing. "I've tried everything: I've walked outside, I've sat by the fire, I've watched TV, I've listened to music, I've tried to relax. But I can't. It won't go away."

I needed to get back to sleep. Morning would come quickly, and with it, three very active little boys. "I want to help you, but it seems like there really isn't anything I can do," I said. He didn't respond. I told him I loved him and lay back down, praying and hoping it would all just go away. "It will be better in the morning," I whispered to myself. "He just needs to sleep."

My boys woke me before sunrise. Still groggy and disoriented from the middle-of-the-night chaos, I peered over to Andrew's side of the bed and saw that he was sound asleep, snoring. *Good,* I thought. *Glad that's over.*

Except it wasn't over. Night after night for the next several months, the same scene would take place in our bedroom. The panic would start in his chest with a dull pain, reminiscent of heartburn or a sore muscle. I'd watch as it settled deeper and completely took over his body. I could tell he was having a panic attack solely by the look in his eyes. His eyes would glaze over, and his pupils would dilate. I would get up close to him, cup his face in my hands, and search for some small glimpse of my Andrew. But time and time again he wasn't there. All I could do in those moments was pray. *God, please take it away. He is suffering, and I am suffering, and we can't live like this anymore.*

I couldn't help but wonder, what was he afraid of? Where was the fear coming from? Why now? My mind went back to October 2017, a difficult month for us. Andrew had undergone two surgeries to remove a softball-sized mass from his chest. We were relieved to hear it was benign, but during the month he was recovering, a close member of our family experienced a significant threat, which I believe may have been the biggest invitation for fear.

When our family member's life was threatened, Andrew took action. After speaking with trained law enforcement professionals, we determined that the only solution to the threat was to move our little family and our beloved family member to a private property behind a gate. A property we would purchase under an alias and surveil by top-of-the-line cameras. It may sound extreme, but at the time it felt necessary. Our family had already walked through immense trauma with the loss of Dave, and we felt protective. Our fragile hearts couldn't take the thought of losing anyone else we loved. We felt if we did this, we would be safe, in our own little compound, our own private retreat, away from any potential danger.

As we searched for a new home, Andrew's panic attacks continued; like a thief in the night, they stole away our sleep, our joy, and our sanity. As the months wore on, I began to feel exhausted and empty. It was like having a newborn baby all over again; no one was sleeping. And Andrew—he wasn't Andrew anymore. Fear was changing him, transforming him. He was beginning to lose who he was as fear took over.

I spent countless hours scrolling through my phone, researching, desperate for answers and solutions. I'd heard about panic attacks before. I'd seen characters in movies breathe into a brown paper sack to stop hyperventilating. In those movies and even in real life, I'd heard the words *panic attack* used lightly, mostly out of context. It seemed like the phrase had been lost and distorted by casual misuse.

In my research I learned a panic attack isn't just a moment of stress or confusion; it's a disorder that can strike suddenly, out of the blue.[1] Panic is fear, a fear so intense it triggers severe physical reactions even though there is no real danger or apparent cause.[2] It's fear gone wild and can only be tamed with treatment, tender care, and time. So we sought help from medical professionals, and Andrew was treated with both natural supplements and low-dose medication.

As I think back to the days of my Andrew wrestling with

crippling fear, I am reminded of one of my favorite books, *Hinds' Feet on High Places* by Hannah Hurnard, which I read after Andrew passed away. It is a beautiful allegory of a girl named Much-Afraid who is on a journey with the Shepherd (God) to the High Places. She sets out with Sorrow and Suffering by her side, and she is consistently attacked and tormented by Craven Fear (the Enemy) along the way. Even though she knows she can call on the Shepherd at any moment, she still allows Craven Fear to play games with her mind. He follows her all the way up to the High Places. With every step she takes, Craven Fear is never far away. At any moment he could show up, stop her in her tracks, and beckon her to turn around and run away from her calling, away from her dreams, away from her future, away from the place God has promised to her, the place where healing and wholeness awaits.

Like Much-Afraid, I felt like fear followed us everywhere. It ran the show, and it was running rampant in our home. As we worked closely with Andrew's doctor, there seemed to be no explanation for the sudden changes in him—the only reasonable conclusion was that Andrew could be suffering from hyperthyroidism. His symptoms seemed to fit the bill: difficulty sleeping, fatigue, heart palpitations, irritability, nervousness, tremors, and weight loss. He was no stranger to this diagnosis; he had experienced a minor episode of hyperthyroidism in high school. We were relieved, and I thought, *This is it! It's just his thyroid. We will find the right specialist to prescribe the right medication, and he will be back to normal in no time.* We made the appointment and waited.

As we waited, Andrew continued to be tortured by fear, which led to continued anxiety and panic attacks. The fear was out of his control. It was deep, and its grip was growing stronger. But he pushed through the pain and continued to show up for work and to preach regularly on Sundays. As a driven, passionate leader, he didn't want to stop, but his body and mind were growing tired, and burnout seemed inevitable. He was running at an unsustainable pace.

Hitting a Wall

Ministry fatigue and burnout aren't uncommon in pastors. One of Andrew's favorite books, *Leading on Empty*, addresses this directly. It was a book Andrew read three or four times, and one that he encouraged our entire family and church staff to read as well. He underlined passages and took notes in the margins on nearly every page. Unfortunately, my eyes didn't meet the words until it was too late—until after Andrew was gone. As I read it after his death, a new empathy and compassion grew in my heart for my precious husband and for other pastors who are pushing themselves to lead from the emptiest place.

In the book, author Wayne Cordeiro shares some statistics he found in H. B. London Jr.'s *Pastors at Greater Risk*. These statistics about pastors are shocking enough that I feel compelled to share them here:

- 75 percent report they've had a significant stress-related crisis at least once in their ministry.

- 50 percent feel unable to meet the needs of the job.
- 90 percent feel they're inadequately trained to cope with ministry demands.
- 45 percent of pastors' wives say the greatest danger to them and their family is physical, emotional, mental, and spiritual burnout.
- 45.5 percent of pastors say that they've experienced depression or burnout to the extent that they needed to take a leave of absence from ministry.
- 70 percent of pastors do not have someone they consider a close friend.[3]

I think sometimes we forget pastors are people too. They aren't superhuman; they're human. And in their humanity, they are susceptible to the same stressors as the rest of us. After years of running hard and fast in ministry, Andrew fell into these statistics. He was physically, emotionally, spiritually, and mentally burned out and unfortunately was never able to recover.

The Final Straw

On Easter weekend in April 2018, Andrew was on the church campus, gearing up to speak for the first of seven services that would stretch over the course of three days. He had just returned home from a three-week trip to India and Uganda, a trip I had attempted to talk him out of, a trip that had already been postponed once due to Andrew's health complications. But he was passionate about the work our church was doing in India and excited about the potential connections to be made in Africa. He felt strongly that his presence on the trip was necessary, so I eventually accepted that there was nothing I could do to prevent him from going.

When he returned, he was as exhausted as I expected. He was still suffering from panic attacks, fear, and anxiety. He was running on empty but somehow would be able to give the Easter message. On the day of the first service, however, a security guard found Andrew curled up on the bathroom floor. He was hyperventilating so badly that he was starting to lose sensation in his hands and feet. The security guard called me and another family member, and we rushed to the office to help. I knew as soon as I locked eyes with Andrew that the fear had taken hold. The same fear I had seen nearly every night for six long months: out of control, untouchable, irrational, and terrifying. *Fear gone wild.*

Andrew's eyes were glazed over, his pupils were dilated, and he was . . . gone. I knew there wasn't much we could do to relieve his pain other than wait it out beside him. We prayed aloud, rubbed his back, and spoke truth over him. I was so relieved when, miraculously, the panic attack subsided just in time for Andrew to be mic'd up and rushed onto the stage.

As he began speaking to the church, I sat in the greenroom, surrounded by the band who had just finished their worship set, and broke into tears. I fell into the arms of the musicians, my friends, and wept. Andrew was onstage speaking, I was backstage crying, and not a single person sitting in the sanctuary could have known anything was amiss. In my heart it all felt so wrong. My faith was weary, and I thought, *Where are you, God? Why aren't you fixing this? Why does he continue to suffer? What am I supposed to do?*

I was tired. I was tired of cohabitating with fear. It lurked around every corner, ready to pounce at any moment. Our life had become more unpredictable than ever. We never knew when a panic attack would strike, and they were happening too often. It seemed like the ugly was outweighing the beautiful, and it was suffocating my heart.

Just a few weeks later, Andrew had a massive panic attack, one we couldn't manage at home. At the hospital, doctors ran new tests on his thyroid and concluded that his blood work was normal. His thyroid looked healthy. There wasn't anything else they could do but send him home with some medication to help him relax. After we arrived home from the hospital, Andrew, our immediate family members, and the lead staff from the church all agreed it was time for him to take an extended break. He was tired, he was burned out, and he needed to rest, recharge, reset, re-something, re-anything—anything but what we were living.

The following Sunday, a few key members from the church board stepped onto the stage and announced Andrew would be taking an unexpected sabbatical. They were honest and explained he had been struggling with anxiety and panic attacks, and the church responded with love and support. We received hundreds of cards, gifts, and prayers, and we were so comforted to know we had a vast army of people cheering us on as we tried to figure out what to do next.

At home during the sabbatical, we believed we'd survived the worst, that the hospital visit, the last panic attack, was as bad as it could get. We had hope that we would figure this out, whatever *this* was, and we would find a way to rise strong again, together. I was a "stand by my man" kind of girl. I was crazy about him. I served him well, I put him first, and I respected and honored him. I knew Andrew was resilient and strong. I was confident God had an incredible plan for his life and believed this was just a small bump in the road. He would get through this. We would get through this. Surely the best was yet to come.

On paper Andrew had everything he could ever want. He was in his dream job. He was leading a large, thriving church at only twenty-nine years old. He had a wife who would follow him to the moon, three beautiful young boys who adored him, a family who would drop anything to be there for him, and we were just a few weeks away from moving into our new private home, a place we all eagerly hoped would bring safety, comfort, and healing.

But what we didn't know was we were stepping into the wilderness. What we believed to be tame, under control, and predictable actually wasn't. We were about to enter into the most trying, exhausting, and confusing season of our lives.

The Wilderness

In the Bible, the word *wilderness* appears more than three hundred times. God's people were constantly in the wilderness, driven there either by flight or fight.

In flight mode, they ran away from their circumstances, from the only home they knew, searching for a safe haven. In fight mode, they wrestled with life, with God, and with their desert surroundings.

Flight and fight are our body's natural reactions to fear. They, along with *freeze*, are physiological reactions to feeling scared. Our body releases hormones that cause us to stay and fight, flee to safety, or freeze, paralyzed by panic. These reactions can be triggered by a real physical threat, such as someone breaking into our home, or a psychological threat, such as giving a speech in public. Interestingly, the symptoms are very similar to those of a panic attack: rapid heartbeat, dilated pupils, pale or flushed skin, and trembling. In fact, a severe case of flight, fight, or freeze can eventually lead to a panic attack.

These fear responses, though discomforting, are actually designed to help us, not harm us. When hormones surge and we begin to tremble, we might feel as though we are losing control of our body. It may feel irritating, foreign, and debilitating, but the reactions increase our chance of survival and the likelihood of us rising victorious from the imposed threat.

Fight, flight, or freeze usually passes quickly, allowing us to return to our normal state of mind. But in some seasons of life, when the fight is long and grueling, when the flight drives us away into isolation, or when we're so overwhelmed that we freeze, we may find ourselves in the wilderness—either by our own accord or by God's divine will. What's beautiful about the wilderness, though, is that God would never allow us to navigate such a wild and unruly place alone. He gave us a friend, a trusted companion, the ultimate survival guide, someone who has gone before and knows the way: the Holy Spirit. Even when the wilderness feels painful, foreign, confusing, vast, and empty, it can also be the place where God does some of his best work.

In the Bible, when Elijah fled in fear to the wilderness, God found him and spoke to him in a whisper. When Hagar ran away and was crying on the side of the road in the wilderness, God sent an angel to encourage her broken heart. When God led Abraham to the wilderness, God made him a great nation and gave him the miraculous gift of a son. When David fled for his life and found himself in the wilderness, God used that time to produce through David scripture that would encourage and influence people for thousands of years. God has consistently allowed his chosen people to be led into the isolation and emptiness of the wilderness.

Perhaps the most memorable wilderness story throughout Scripture is Jesus' journey through the wild. Even God in the flesh found himself in the most desolate place. But prior to his wandering for forty days, Jesus experienced a monumental moment.

> Then Jesus left Galilee to come to the Jordan to be baptized by John. But when he waded into the water, John resisted him, saying, "Why are you doing this? I'm the one who needs to be baptized by you, and yet you come to be baptized by me?"
>
> Jesus replied, "It is only right to do all that God requires." Then John baptized Jesus. And as Jesus rose up out of the water, the heavenly realm opened up over him and he saw the Holy Spirit descend out of the heavens and rest upon him in the form of a dove. (Matt. 3:13–17 TPT)

In this powerful moment, God, the Holy Spirit, and Jesus began a new kind of ministry here on earth. God could have left Jesus alone, but instead God sent him a helper, a comforter, a guide, an intercessor, a friend who would play an invaluable part in the life and ministry of Jesus. A foreshadowing of what God would do for us all. Whether we find ourselves in the dark, lonely places of the valley or in the bright, warm sun on the mountaintop, we can draw comfort from the fact that, just like Jesus, we never wander alone.

Immediately following Jesus' baptism, the Spirit led him into the desert wilderness. A pattern we see throughout the Scripture is that right after a significant spiritual event, just when it seems like victory or maturity has been attained, temptations resume more strongly than ever.[4] Jesus understood this and knew that his time in the wilderness wasn't pointless. Instead it served a valuable purpose. "Remember how the LORD your God led you all the way in the wilderness these forty years, to humble and test you in order to know what was in your heart, whether or not you would keep his commands" (Deut. 8:2).

The wilderness has a beautiful way of prying open our hearts. As we wander through the wide-open spaces, we discover who we really are and how great our need for God really is. The wilderness isn't optional; it's an integral part of life. We all walk through tragedies and trials, and we have either gone through, are going through, or will go through, something painful.

Maybe, like me, you planned out your life, but it didn't pan out the way you wanted it to.

Maybe the promotion you thought was coming never came.
Maybe the dream you had in mind never became a reality.
Maybe there was a relapse instead of remission.
Maybe there was a divorce instead of reconciliation.
Maybe you want to start a family, and though you've been
trying for years, your arms are still empty.
Maybe you deeply desire to be married, and though you've
gone on date after date, you are still single.
Maybe you were enjoying a stable, happy life and then mental
illness came out of nowhere, and now you find yourself
sitting in a season of depression that is dark, terrifying, and
debilitating. And maybe for the first time ever, you are wrestling
with suicidal thoughts that you never thought you would have.

Time in the wilderness will come for us all, but it doesn't have to ruin our lives. With the supernatural strength and peace that can only come from the Divine, I truly believe we can survive and even thrive in the empty places. To remind myself of this hope, I've hung a green metal sign in my kitchen right above the stove. I read it every morning and believe every word. It says, "You are braver than you believe, stronger than you seem, smarter than you think, and loved more than you'll ever know." Every word is true. Our most hated circumstances do not define us. We are not what has happened to us or within us. Our worth is found in him who sees past all the mess, the chaos, the exterior façade and looks straight at the heart. Even on our worst day he calls us precious, honored, and loved. And maybe that's all we need to hear today.

You are precious.
You are honored.
You are loved.

All we have is today. And every moment of today rests in his mighty hands. If he wants to carry us home tomorrow, he will. If he wants to lead us into the wild, he will. If he wants to bless our lives and give us favor, he will. He sees the bigger picture; he sees straight into our hearts, and he knows exactly what's waiting for us on the other side of the wilderness.

THREE

How Did We End Up Here?

Your husband has depression." Those four words altered our lives forever.

I couldn't muster a response to the pronouncement. I sat stunned. The psychiatrist glanced at me, then back down at the papers strewn about his desk. He was an older man, on the verge of retirement. He was well respected, well known, very kind, and had taken a liking to Andrew right away. Andrew knew the doctor liked him because he always placed Andrew as the last appointment of the day, so they could have more time together. The doctor truly believed in Andrew, and I knew I had to lean into his knowledge and experience because we couldn't fix this on our own. Professional help was part of the sabbatical plan, but I wasn't prepared for this.

"Andrew is on the low end of the spectrum. We are going to help him rest, and he will bounce right back. You don't need to worry. I am very confident your husband is going to be just fine." I didn't speak. I wanted to leave; I wanted to escape this moment and pretend it never happened. The doctor wrote a few prescriptions—one for anxiety, one for sleep, one for depression—and handed them to Andrew, then sent us on our way. Outside his office, my mind was spinning. I'd anticipated a quick appointment, in and out, like most doctor's appointments, and looked forward to our date night afterward. But those four words, *your husband has depression*, had disrupted my world.

A mountain of thoughts grew in my mind. *Could we have avoided all of this? Isn't this a bit dramatic? How is this my life? Is he sure Andrew is actually* depressed?

It was a hot day in late April as we slid into Andrew's black sports car and turned on the AC, but I continued to melt from the inside out. My tears were visible now, streaming rapidly down my cheeks. I kept my head down. I didn't want to see his face; I didn't want to face any of this.

Andrew placed his hand on my thigh, gave it a couple gentle pats, and took a deep breath. "What's wrong, Kayla? Look at me. Why are you crying? What's going on?"

The panic attacks were one thing, but an actual depression diagnosis, coupled with actual depression medication, was all too real, all too heavy, all too much for my mind to comprehend. I lifted my head to look at the man I loved, the man I would do anything for, the man who held my heart in the palm of his hands. He was wearing a pair of ripped-up jeans and a button-down shirt. His hair had been perfectly gelled and combed, not a single strand out of place. He was always handsome and well kept. I thought back to all the Saturday afternoons when Andrew had strolled through Nordstrom Rack, searching for a new pair of shoes or a new shirt to wear as he spoke to the congregation on Sunday. After shopping, once the boys were tucked into bed, he'd give himself a fresh haircut and then hand the clippers over to me to trim the hairs on the back of his neck. Then he'd stand in his long brown robe in our walk-in closet, staring at the clothes draped from the wooden hangers. Methodically, he would pick out each piece of his outfit for the next day, all the way down to his shoes. Sometimes he would try on a few things, asking my opinion. "How does this look? Do these shoes go with this shirt? Which pair of pants do you like better?"

After making his selection, he would pull out the ironing board, heat up the iron, and slowly melt away every single crease and wrinkle. Finally, when he was finished he would crawl into bed, and I would snuggle up next to him, drape my arm across his strong body, press my cheek against his chest, and listen to his heartbeat. My head would rise and fall with his breaths; he was so beautifully alive. For a minute or two, we would just lie there together, not speaking because together was enough. Then I would pray. Every single Saturday night I would pray. I would sit up, lay one hand on his chest, and with the other hand I would run my fingers through his coarse brown hair. His whole body would relax and melt into the bed. I would say amen, we would kiss good night, and we would each roll to our side of the bed and drift off to sleep together, me and my guy, as one.

I loved Saturday nights because they were predictable. I knew what to expect, I knew what was expected of me, and I knew how much Saturday night mattered because Sunday was coming. For our family, Sunday was the most important day of the week. But we lost the days of predictability when the panic attacks started and now *depression*? All of these thoughts, all of these memories, flashed through my mind as we sat in the hot parking lot. I longed to go back to our usual Saturday nights, to the days when the expectations were clear and life made sense. *What happened to my husband? Who is this man sitting next to me?*

I hardly recognized him.

I placed my hand on Andrew's, gripped it tight, found his tired blue eyes with my hazel ones, and whispered through my tears, "How did we end up here?"

Andrew drew back as if startled by my response. "What do you mean?" His expression spoke a hundred words. I could tell he was confused, but I needed to be honest.

"How did we end up in a psychiatrist's office?" I asked. "How did we get here? How did you wind up with depression? The psychiatrist just looked me in the eyes and told me you have *depression*. How did this happen?" I was talking so quickly that I could barely get the words out. All of the stressful weeks and months leading up to this moment came bubbling to the surface. I had erupted, unable to hold back my emotions anymore. I stared down at my feet, ashamed of my feelings and wishing I could be strong for him. I wanted to look him in the eyes and tell him that everything was going to be okay. He was supposed to be the one falling apart, not me. He was the one who was sick; his was the name the doctor had written on the prescriptions.

Naturally, Andrew kept his composure as he readjusted himself in his seat. I could tell by his pause he was premeditating his words before he said them out loud.

"Kayla, it's going to be okay. This is a good thing." Another pause, another deep breath. I could feel him looking at me, but I didn't raise my head. I closed my eyes to block it all out, but I heard his voice, calm and soothing, say, "I'm on the low end of the spectrum. I'm going to bounce back, we are going to be all right. Kayla, please look at me."

I mustered up the courage to lift my head and found his eyes again.

"I love you, Kayla. We'll do this together. I'm actually relieved to have a diagnosis. They finally know what's wrong with me. I'm going to be okay. Let's get out of here, 'kay?"

I reluctantly nodded my head. I wanted to believe him. I wanted to be hopeful, but I wasn't.

We went to dinner at our favorite Mexican restaurant, a place where the chance of running into people from church was slim, a place where we could relax and enjoy our time together without interruption. Dinner was short and quiet. My mind was somewhere else, wandering through the future, worrying about how this new diagnosis was going to affect us all. What about the boys? What about the church? What about our new home? What if he didn't get better?

On the way home, we stopped by the pharmacy to fill his prescriptions. We left with a small plastic bag containing a few green bottles of pills, each with the power to change the mind completely, each promising just as much risk as reward. They might work, or they might not. They could take away his depression and anxiety, or they could make it worse. They could cause his emotions to ramp up, or they could numb him out completely. They could release new joy, or they could cause suicidal thoughts. Despite the little bit of knowledge I had about potential side effects, these medications were a mystery. I was overwhelmed by this new journey down a new road, but even though I was a reluctant passenger, I was along for the ride. And all the while I continued asking myself, *How did we end up here*?

Depression wasn't a foreign term to me. I'd studied it in college while earning my bachelor's degree in psychology. I had friends and family members who had struggled with it, but in the back of my mind, I held major misconceptions. I thought people with depression had a flair for the dramatic. I dumbed down depression as an excuse for laziness. When a friend with postpartum depression checked out in her bedroom while her husband changed diapers and fed the baby, I thought, *How could she do that to her family?* I viewed depression through the lens of criticism and cynicism.

What I failed to understand is that depression is not a choice. It's not something that a person can control by willpower any more than someone with the flu can just choose to feel better. It can happen to anyone, at any time, for any reason. Andrew did not choose depression; it chose him. His life circumstances, fatigue, and a genetic predisposition put him in a fragile state, and his mind fell victim to the darkness of depression. He needed medical attention from medical professionals, and he needed medical prescriptions.

As I watched Andrew during his most intense battles, I could tell he felt trapped by his own mind. I read somewhere that people struggling with depression feel like they are drowning while everyone else around them is breathing. It's a suffocating darkness that isolates, confuses, and exhausts.

If he could have found a way to the surface to catch his breath, I know Andrew would have. He often made subtle comments about his condition with the undertone of feeling deeply misunderstood by family and friends. Though we were trying to help, we often felt just as confused as Andrew. The depression was changing him; it was changing all of us. As he wrestled with his depression, new behaviors and emotions came to the surface that sometimes resulted in words or actions completely out of character for Andrew, even self-sabotaging.

Living with Depressed Andrew felt like walking on eggshells much of the time. I never knew which version of Andrew was going to come out of our bedroom in the morning. Would he be happy? Sad? Angry? Tired? Would he be present with the kids, or would I have to parent another day alone?

Almost every day the answer was different. I lived in the tension of caretaker and mother, constantly torn between carrying for Andrew's needs and tending to the needs of our three boys, ages two, four, and five at the time. Emotions were high, peace was absent, the future was foggy, the questions were never-ending, and fear was ever present. Every ounce of me wanted to be with Andrew: lying in bed with him all day, running my fingers through his hair, whispering in his ear, "Everything is going to be okay," praying over him, going with him to doctor's appointments. But I couldn't. Our boys needed their mom, and I felt like a single parent. My heart began to harden.

We were lost in the wilderness with seemingly no way out. I would walk around my home and whisper under my breath in desperation, "I hate my life." I would scroll through Instagram and see other people enjoying life together, and resentment and bitterness would grow in my heart. *Why can't we get back to normal?* I'd think. I'd look at those families going on camping trips, taking their kids to Disneyland, and spending time at the beach while I was trapped in a circumstance that I couldn't change. I'd wonder if Andrew would ever get better, and I'd cry out in prayer, "Where are you God? Why are you allowing this to happen?"

What Do We Do About Depression?

What I learned from our long, exhausting summer is that the dark cloud of depression doesn't just block out the light for the afflicted. It also blocks out the light for those who love them the most. For a while, life loses its color as the darkness touches everything. And our experience is not a rare occurrence. Andrew was just one out of the 17.3 million estimated cases of adult depression diagnosed each year in the United States.[1] As instances of mental illness, including depression and suicide, steadily increase, we need to remember that none of us are exempt. Not the friendly neighbor who always waves, the teen football star, the mom with the perfectly curated Instagram feed, or the pastor with beautiful potential and so much to live for. We are surrounded by people in pain, and the way we respond to their pain matters. We can all open our eyes a little wider and work a little harder to truly see one another. We are all capable of taking bigger steps out of our comfortable lives to love and help those who are living in pain.

A common misconception in Christian culture is that

depression is somehow linked to sin and spirituality, but I came to realize that it doesn't happen because of a lack of prayer, time spent in the Bible, or faith. I now know that depression is a real physical illness that needs to be treated with professional help, tender care, empathy, and compassion. One of the most painful things a follower of Jesus can do is openly criticize the faith of a person who is in the darkness of depression. Even with the best intentions, if we aren't careful with our words, we could heap more shame and sorrow upon our friends who are mentally ill.

It's my hope and prayer that we will change the conversation and break the stigma, that we will find new ways to replace the old approaches to mental illness. There are four powerful words my mother-in-law, Carol, shared in a message to our church that I believe can help us see another person's pain more clearly. These words have the ability to change our hearts and stop us from thinking or saying something critical and potentially untrue. These are the words she shared: *I have no idea.*[2]

I have no idea about their story or history.
I have no idea what burdens they are carrying.
I have no idea what it's like to live with what they are living with.
I have no idea what's going on inside their mind.
I have no idea about their mental illness.
I have no idea.

I find that to be incredibly convicting. We have no idea what it's like to walk in anyone else's shoes but our own. And this is especially true when it comes to mental health issues. I believe there are more effective ways we can walk alongside and support someone who is suffering.

LISTEN WITHOUT JUDGMENT

Oftentimes people battling depression are confused about their own emotions. If we create space for them to process their emotions out loud, it may actually help minimize their pain and provide clarity. It can also open the door for us to respond to their thoughts and feelings with empathy instead of advice. By listening and responding with words like, "I hear you, and I am so sorry for your pain" or "It must be so hard to feel the way you feel" or "Please know I'm here for you no matter what; we will get through this together," we create space for healing to begin. When we realize our job isn't to fix the depression, we can begin to sit with those we love in their pain.

ENGAGE, DON'T IGNORE

Battling depression often leads to isolation because normal, everyday things like going to the grocery store, going to work, spending time with friends, and even getting out of bed can feel overwhelming and unbearable. Unlike normal fatigue, depression is an exhaustion that does not go away—no matter how much caffeine is consumed, how much sleep is had, or how many vitamins are swallowed. The best thing we can do for our loved ones struggling with depression is to keep engaging them. They may not answer our phone calls, respond to our text messages, or open the door when we stop by, but we can't give up. If we give up, it may lead them to give up too.

Instead we can keep showing up; we can keep showing them that there is nothing they can do to push us away. If they don't answer the phone, we can leave them encouraging voicemails; if they don't answer the door, we can leave special gifts or thoughtful notes on their doorsteps. We can continue to show up because their lives are worth fighting for.

ENCOURAGE SELF-CARE

People who are walking through the darkness of depression may have lost the desire or ability to care for themselves. As a way to encourage self-care, we can sit beside them and help create a list of things that bring them joy. It doesn't have to be complicated; self-care can be as simple as going for a walk, cooking a yummy meal, riding a bike around the block, watching a show on Netflix, or reading a good book. Self-care may even be something we can do together with our loved ones until they're strong enough to do it on their own.

PRAY

One of the most important things we can do for someone with depression is pray—and do it in a way that doesn't minimize our loved ones' pain but instead reminds them that they are not alone. We can pray with them and for them just like we would pray for a friend battling cancer. If they refuse to pray together, we can pray from a distance, fighting and interceding for our loved ones who may be too run-down to fight for themselves. Prayer may not always lead to miraculous healing; the healing isn't up to us. Sometimes God sends supernatural miracles, and sometimes he simply says no or wait. Maybe in the wilderness of waiting for prayers to be answered we'll be reminded that true faith isn't about being dazzled by miracles. True faith is about being faithful—no matter the outcome.

The Wilderness

Depression isn't new; throughout history we see stories of real people plagued with real seasons of depression. I find comfort in the fact that the heroes of our faith had their own dark moments of overwhelming pain. Pain that drove them to the isolation of the wilderness and to the edge of their mortality. Pain that oftentimes came after a mountaintop moment of faith.

As Jesus stepped away from his baptism and into the wilderness, I wonder what thoughts were swirling in his mind. He was fully God, yet fully human, and in his humanity he was filled with real thoughts, real emotions, a real beating heart—fully alive. He knew the Spirit was leading him to the wilderness to be tested, but I often wonder how he felt. Was he afraid, or was he fearless? Was he filled with joy, or was he depressed? Was he anxious or peaceful? No matter his mental state, he remained obedient. He allowed the Father, through the Spirit, to lead him into the wild unknown (Matt. 4:1).

Perhaps Jesus knew this would be part of the plan all along. Genesis 22 reveals that God tested Abraham by asking him to offer his son as a sacrifice. Abraham, in faith, remained obedient to God, and in the final hour God spared his son's life. Job 1:6 explains that God allowed Satan to test Job, a man of integrity and deep reverence for God. Satan took everything away from Job: his wealth, his health, his family, and his friends, until he was left alone in the dirt in deep physical, emotional, and spiritual pain. But Job remained faithful to God, and at the very end of Job's story, we see God restore his life and double his fortune.

Both Abraham and Job had every reason to turn and walk away from their faith. But they didn't. Instead they trusted God—even in the face of death, even when it seemed ludicrous in the eyes of the world. They said yes to him when they could have said no. They kept a tight grip on their faith when it would have been easy to give up or reach out for something or someone else to save them.

Whether the pain we are facing today is physical or mental, or both, we can choose to keep putting one foot in front of the other, knowing that even in our deepest pain, God is still near. I will never fully understand why God allows the darkness of depression to plague minds. I'll never fully grasp why some people are healed and others aren't. But what I do understand is that even if the darkness lasts a lifetime, we have all been promised a place in heaven where freedom and healing are forever. And maybe our dark days here will feel small and insignificant as we stand in the light of eternity. In the meantime, in the wilderness of the world, where the pain is real and deep, we can continue to walk in faith. We can ask God to teach us how to embrace and live with the pain, and we can press on through every trial knowing the finish line is near.

FOUR

To the Back
of the Cave

Have you ever heard of silverback gorillas?" the therapist asked, looking at each of us and waiting for a response. We had been seeing this therapist for two hours every week since the beginning of the sabbatical, but this session was different. Andrew and I looked at each other, a little puzzled about why she was bringing up gorillas in our counseling session.

I shook my head and said, "No, why?"

Her face lit up, her eyes opened wide, and she leaned in close, as if to let us in on a secret. "Silverback gorillas are incredible creatures. They travel in groups, and each group has an alpha male. The alpha male works tirelessly to gather up food for his family, and once he's exhausted from all of his work, he finds a cave and goes to the back of the cave to sleep. He doesn't tell any of the other gorillas where he's going. He doesn't worry about his family. He simply does what he needs to do to preserve his own energy and stops everything to rest."

I knew where her example was going. She was about to encourage Andrew to be like the gorilla and go to the back of a cave. My mind roiled, and I wanted to snap, "But what about me! I'm tired too! I'm the one taking care of him and the kids! I'm the one who needs a cave!"

But I didn't. I didn't say anything. I took a deep breath and waited for her to say the words. And she did. "Andrew, you need to run to the back of a cave." He sighed, and his whole body seemed to melt into the worn floral couch. With tears in his eyes, he gave a resounding nod.

After that session and over the next few weeks, the phrase *back of the cave* became Andrew's code for "I'm going to the bedroom to rest." I did all I could to help. I removed any pressure at home and gave him the space and freedom to focus on his health. That freedom and the advice from the counselor cracked open the door for Andrew to give himself permission to rest, something he had struggled to do for years.

It made sense. He had been running hard and fast for a long time. He had led our family and our church through four very difficult years leading up to the death of his father, and now, almost three years later, it was all catching up with him. His body had run out of fuel. Much like the silverback gorilla, Andrew needed some downtime, some alone time, some no-pressure time to just be still. To recharge his adrenals and reclaim his life. He knew and I knew that if he was ever going to return to work, he would need to take full advantage of this time. So he did.

On paper we were doing everything we knew to create space for Andrew's healing. He was seeing the psychiatrist biweekly, and we were seeing the counselor together for two hours every week. He was also seeing a wellness doctor, who recommended numerous vitamins and supplements to boost his energy and increase his overall health. He was getting plenty of rest in his "cave," and he was working out every single day to rebuild muscle and regain strength. He would also occasionally retreat to the desert or the mountains to be alone with God, and sometimes the boys and I would join him. We did not want to squander his sabbatical; we took the time seriously. We were a team.

Halfway through the summer, Andrew and I took a two-week road trip together, just the two of us—a trip I will hold close to my heart for the rest of my life. We had been married for nearly eight years, and this vacation reminded both of us that we not only loved each other but also liked each other.

Our adventure started from our home in Southern California and ended in the beautiful mountains of Park City, Utah. We took a few days to get there, even stopping over in Vegas to celebrate my twenty-ninth birthday with dinner and a show. Our final destination was a condo overlooking the gorgeous tree-covered hills of Park City.

There is one day in particular I go back to again and again in my mind. I called it "Andrew's adventure day." We rented a dune buggy and went off-roading through the mountains. It was a perfect day to explore, with clear blue skies and warm sunshine. The motor hummed loudly as we sped through the thick green trees. Stunning streaks of light came beaming through the branches as we held hands and adventured onto trails unknown. I remember saying through happy tears, "This place feels like heaven." Andrew was also happy, the happiest I had seen him in a long time. A genuine smile spread across his face all day. I had missed his smile, I had missed his laugh, I had missed his joy. We spent the whole day in that buggy, splashing through giant mud puddles, taking sharp turns on high cliffs, enjoying the beauty of our surroundings and the gift of doing it together. It was a stark contrast to the dark days of our valley season.

That day was an absolute gift to me. It was quite literally a mountaintop moment. It gave me hope that things could get better, that joy wasn't far out of reach, that we could find happiness if we looked hard enough. I believed he would find his joy again, the darkness would fade, and there would be more dune-buggy days to come. I just had to hold on and hold him through this season.

But when we returned home, Andrew withdrew to his cave, to the dark place of depression, confusion, and isolation. He rested in our bedroom most days, and even when he was present with me and the kids, his mind seemed disconnected, lost somewhere else. I continued to encourage him to do whatever he needed to heal. I poured out everything I had for him and our kids, clinging to the hope we would see healing soon. Leaning into God, leaning into the season, I pushed through the daily pain.

The rest of the summer crept along. We had moved into our new house. Now, by our own choosing and intense planning, we were living on a large private property behind a gate, away from "the world." It's no wonder we felt like no one really understood what was going on in our home, what we were going through, what we were living every day. We felt alone because most days we were. I wish I could say our home was flooded with family, friends, and invitations to summer barbecues, but it wasn't. Most days it was just the five of us—Andrew, me, and our three little boys—taking it one day at a time together.

In my mind I blamed the lack of connection with others on Andrew's illness. I assumed it made people feel uncomfortable, an assumption likely stemming from my own misconceptions of depression. I, too, felt uncomfortable, even in my own home. I struggled to know who to confide in, who to reach out to, and who to invite into our pain. For the majority of my friends, Andrew was their pastor, so I didn't want them to see him as weak, sick, or sad. I wanted to keep his image strong. I was worried if I opened up and told even my closest friends what was really going on, they would lose respect for him.

In other words, I let fear be my friend instead of my actual friends. I chose fear over freedom and isolation over community, and I began to slowly unravel. I was growing weary, and my mind was falling into a darkness and depression of its own. Bitterness began to creep into my heart. I was frustrated with God; I didn't understand why he hadn't yet lifted the darkness. I felt hopeless, my prayers felt useless, and I wondered if God even cared.

Ironically, Andrew and I were both living in isolation, him in "the back of the cave" and me in the protection of our home. I hardly left our property. It was beautiful, an oasis of mature eucalyptuses, pines, and pepper trees, complete with a dual-waterfall river, outdoor fireplace, and giant dirt lot for the boys to be boys. While Andrew rested and worked on his health, the boys and I would play. We held races on bike paths with jumps we built in the dirt; we chased bad guys in cop cars in the driveway; we boogie boarded down the Slip 'N Slide on the grass in the backyard and lay out by the kiddie pool imagining we were at the beach.

When bedtime rolled around I was completely exhausted. Most days Andrew would come out of his cave to help with bedtime, but as soon as the boys were in bed he would return. Many nights I would stay in the living room and sit on the couch alone. An introvert at heart, I needed some time by myself to rest and to check out of my responsibilities.

We continued to wander in our own lonely wildernesses for months. Andrew often felt like no one understood what he was going through, and I, in a different way, felt the same. We were both screaming on the inside, unable to effectively articulate our feelings and express our true emotions, so we isolated from the world—and in some ways from each other.

Isolation vs. Solitude

Sadly, the isolation we experienced isn't uncommon. Many people who suffer from mental illness experience deep isolation. I've learned through our journey that isolation isn't the same thing as solitude. Isolation is lonely, empty, and dark, while solitude, in the right amounts, can be intentional, life-giving, and soul filling. The only similarity is that they both imply being alone.

Solitude comes from a deep inner longing, and it's something we have to actively seek out. Solitude is fuel for the soul; it's sacred, intentional time to reflect on life away from a busy schedule of responsibilities. It's time set apart to rediscover who we are and find our unique voices again without other voices chiming in.

It's time to sit with God and pour out our hearts to him through prayer. Although we are alone in solitude, we are still connected to God, and solitude helps us connect with ourselves so that we can connect to others.

Isolation, on the other hand, is rooted in disconnection. Isolation doesn't connect us to anyone—not God, ourselves, or others. Isolation isn't active; it's passive. It's staying home alone and binging on Netflix. It's choosing not to participate in activities with friends. It's choosing not to answer the phone and engage in community. Isolation is marked by utter loneliness, while solitude is a state of being alone without being lonely. When we break away for a time of solitude, we can, through introspection, gain fresh self-awareness, but when we spend too much time in isolation, we can actually lose ourselves.

WHY SOLITUDE IS IMPORTANT:

Silences the noise.

Our world is loud. It's easy to go through an entire day without a moment of quiet calm. Most of us wake up and immediately turn on the TV or listen to our smart devices, or we pick up our smartphones and start scrolling, and we fall asleep the same way. We are addicted to noise; it's part of our culture, part of everyday life. Solitude creates space to completely silence the noise. It is a time to be still, to turn off our electronics, to put aside all of the distractions we are bombarded with every single day and instead open up our minds and our hearts for reflection. It is a time to breathe deeply, with open hands, releasing all of our worries, stress, and anxiety. Silence creates space for us to hear the Voice of reason, the only Voice that matters, the still, quiet Voice that is all too often drowned out by overwhelming noise.

Connects us to God through prayer.

Jesus modeled this for us so well. All throughout his ministry Jesus repeatedly left the crowds and went away to pray (Luke 5:16). He even instructed us to pray this way. "Here's what I want you to do: Find a quiet, secluded place so you won't be tempted to role-play before God. Just be there as simply and honestly as you can manage. The focus will shift from you to God, and you will begin to sense his grace" (Matt. 6:6 THE MESSAGE).

Prayer is our fuel and our lifeline between heaven and earth. Through prayer we are able to tap into the supernatural, the infinite, the divine. Without prayer we are all running on empty. C. S. Lewis put it best when he said, "God designed the human machine to run on Himself. He Himself is the fuel our spirits were designed to burn, or the food our spirits were designed to feed on. There is no other."[1] Our souls need prayer like our bodies need oxygen. When we tuck ourselves away in a quiet place to pray, we may be surprised by all God has to say.

Enhances our relationships with others.

We spend our days surrounded by people. Whether virtually or physically, our connection to others in the modern-day world is unparalleled in the history of humankind. This constant connection and stimulation can lead us to disconnect from ourselves. But when we seek solitude, we make the choice to disconnect. When we intentionally spend time alone, we find who we are again, the person we've been since the beginning, the person we were always created to be, the person we might have lost along the way. Self-discovery happens by spending time reflecting on our lives: our ambitions, our goals, our core motivations, our true feelings, our big dreams, without judgment or criticism from others.

Solitude will not happen unless we make time for it. Maybe the best gift we could give ourselves is to pull out the calendar and schedule it right now. Maybe we pencil in a personal retreat day, or maybe if we can't get away for a whole day, we schedule in time during our lunch break. Maybe solitude can be as simple as scheduling one day a week where we disconnect from social media to silence the noise. Or maybe our only time for solitude is in the morning before anyone else in the house is awake. I personally love the quiet calm of the morning. I love waking up before the sun to spend a few hours alone. It's now a routine. I began after I had my third son, after I realized that if I didn't make time to replenish my soul at the beginning of the day, it would never happen. Although it was hard at first, I continued to get up and show up, and I began to see how a quiet soul changed me. I was more connected, more present, and more aware of the presence of God throughout the day.

WHY ISOLATION IS DANGEROUS:
Isolation and loneliness.

We all experience seasons of loneliness in life. Loneliness can stem from a variety of life experiences: the death of a loved one, living alone for the first time, physical health challenges, mental illness (depression or anxiety), fear, or even a lack of purpose. When we walk through the valley of loneliness, we have a more difficult time connecting with others, which can lead us to social isolation. Researchers have found a higher level of social isolation typically leads to higher levels of loneliness;[2] it's a slippery slope down a dangerous path. We need each other; we need real authentic relationships with others where we truly feel known.

Isolation and overall health.

Isolation can cause severe physical health complications. Studies have shown that lack of social connection can increase the risk of death; conversely, individuals' odds of survival increase by at least 50 percent when they maintain social relationships, while in some cases the odds of survival can exceed 90 percent.[3] Social isolation has also been linked to higher blood pressure, cardiovascular disease, vulnerability to infection, difficulty sleeping, and mental health complications, including early onset dementia, depression, and difficulty processing thoughts and logic.[4]

The best question we can ask ourselves when we are sitting alone is: *Am I sitting in solitude or isolation?* If the answer is isolation, it may help to gently acknowledge this so we can work toward healing and building healthy connections again.

Connection doesn't have to be complicated. It could simply be picking up the phone and calling a family member or friend we haven't talked to in a while. Or it could be lacing up our shoes and walking out of the house. Sometimes being outside, or being around other people, even strangers, can be healing. Or if we have no idea where to begin, we could start with a great therapist. A simple Google search or a search on www.psychologytoday.com is an easy way to get connected with a local licensed professional.

The Wilderness

When we spend time in solitude, we can sit with everything we are holding and discover we don't have to hold it alone. Maybe the best way we can prepare for the wilderness seasons of life is to first discover the power of surrender. When Jesus walked into the wilderness, he did so in surrender. He surrendered his body and his mind by fasting forty days and forty nights (Matt. 4:2). We can prepare in the same way Jesus did. For him, fasting was strength training. It was a way of saying to his body, "You are not in charge of me." It's exercise for the soul. It's not about punishment; it's about presence. It's about going without something to create space for Someone. Jesus may have denied himself food for forty days, but he was feasting on the presence and the power of God.

One truth Jesus was well aware of, as we are today, is that the wilderness is temporary. I don't know about you, but I don't want to waste a single day. I deeply believe there is a way to thrive in the wilderness. I believe there is a way to feel every ounce of pain and funnel it into purpose. Although we may find ourselves in the waiting room of the wilderness, it may be where we come to the end of ourselves and, like Jesus, surrender everything as we learn to draw our strength from the only divine source of life. Maybe as we live in daily surrender, we will discover this life was never ours to begin with. Our one life is part of a much bigger story, a beautiful redemptive love story, and we can rest and breathe deeply knowing the Author of every life is in control.

One of my favorite ways to practice surrender is through breath prayer, a form of contemplative prayer that follows the rhythm of our breathing. It's a powerful tool to ease stress and anxiety. When we pay attention to the gentle filling and emptying of our lungs, we slowly shift our minds from swirling, cluttered chaos to powerful peace. We can say the words of our prayer out loud, or we can whisper them in our hearts; either way the practice of breath prayer is centering and grounding. It's as easy as this: inhale a name of God (any name you feel comfortable with), then exhale a need (anything you need). It's short and simple yet sacred. For example:

Inhale, "Jesus," exhale, "help me."
Inhale, "Lord," exhale, "lead me."
Inhale, "Yahweh," exhale, "heal me."
Inhale, "Abba Father," exhale, "let me feel your love."

When we connect with God throughout the day, we can be better prepared for anything that comes our way. Through living a life of surrender, we just might find the small things in life grow smaller as perspective shines light on what truly matters. We were delicately placed right where we are, even in the most painful of circumstances, for such a time as this. And we serve a loving Father who will never abandon us in the wilderness. His outstretched hand is always there to gently lead us through one day, one hour, one breath at a time into the everlasting exhale of eternity.

FIVE

Stranger Things

'll never forget our one-year wedding anniversary. Andrew's parents surprised us with a one-night stay at the Langham, a prestigious hotel in charming downtown Pasadena, California, as our anniversary gift. We were young, broke newlyweds, so it was a huge upgrade from our small, cluttered apartment. The tall, historic building was surrounded by acres of beautiful landscaping. We were walking on air as we checked into our room, giddy even, holding hands, full of anticipation for a special night together. Joy felt close; fear felt miles away.

We dropped off our bags in our room, changed into our fancy clothes, and headed downstairs for dinner. Dinner was delectable, and the waitstaff went above and beyond to make the night special for us, surprising us with champagne and a dessert plate adorned with a chocolate-lettered "happy anniversary." It was picture perfect. We were madly in love, crazy about each other, and the night kept getting better.

After dinner we went back to our room. Andrew wanted to take a shower, so I turned on the TV to watch a show. Then something changed. Joy began to slip away, and fear filled the atmosphere.

I heard a noise that, at first, I thought was coming from the TV, but the noise grew louder. I pressed the Mute button and realized it wasn't the TV at all. "Drew, is that you?" My stomach sank, my heart began to race as my body filled with fear. Why was he crying? What in the world was going on?

I rushed into the bathroom, pulled back the shower curtain, and there he was, on the floor of the shower, curled up in the fetal position, shaking, terrified, and crying hysterically. "Andrew? Oh my God, Andrew! What's wrong? What's going on? What happened?" I was stunned and confused. How could everything shift so radically? I knelt down on the floor next to the tub and began to gently rub his back. The water was still running; streams of water rolled down his back as tears ran down his face.

My mind immediately went to his dad, Dave, who had been diagnosed with aggressive leukemia just a few weeks earlier and was in the middle of fighting for his life in the hospital. Maybe Andrew was just having an emotional moment. Grief can be unpredictable. But I quickly realized that this wasn't grief. This was different. Andrew wasn't sad; he was scared. When he finally calmed down enough to talk, he described in detail an encounter he'd had with a dark presence he called a "creature." I stopped rubbing his back. Full of confusion and fear, I sat on the cold tile floor, unsure what to do next. I began to look around the room. I didn't see any "creature."

"What do you mean a 'creature'? Andrew, what are you talking about? There isn't anything in the shower. You were the only one in here; I don't understand." He started crying again and shaking. I wasn't helping. I was making it worse. So I did the only thing I knew to do—I prayed. "God, I don't know what's going on, but I pray your presence would overwhelm this room right now. Whatever Andrew saw, I pray in the name of Jesus for it to leave; it has no power here. In Jesus' mighty name, amen."

I turned off the shower, grabbed a towel from the counter, and slowly helped Andrew stand to his feet. I carefully wrapped the towel around him and held his body close to mine as we walked toward the bed. "Are you okay? What do you need? What can I do for you?"

He pulled the covers up over his body, closed his eyes, took a long, deep breath, and then opened them again. "I'm okay. That was really scary. I'm still confused, but I feel better. Thank you for praying for me—that really helped."

What was supposed to be a night to remember had quickly turned into a night I hoped I would forget.

Darkness and Light

I grew up going to church. I read stories about the spiritual realm in the Bible, and I believe it is all real. But Andrew's experience had been too real, too close to home. I wish I could say he never had another encounter with darkness, but I can't. Throughout our marriage, Andrew continued to be taunted relentlessly. Sometimes Andrew would tell me about it, but other times he wouldn't. Maybe he even felt like he couldn't. Maybe he didn't want to acknowledge it was real either. He was burdened by a darkness difficult to fully understand.

Every day there is an invisible war raging all around us. A war between good and evil, darkness and light, and we live in the tension. As different people with different upbringings, we may have different understandings of darkness and demons, but I think most people agree there is evil in this world, and it is truly dark. I learned through Scripture to refer to the ruler of the darkness as the devil or the Enemy. In my mind, the Enemy's desire is simple: to replace the light, God's beauty and love, with darkness.

The darkness and the light we encounter are supernatural. They are often unexplainable because they are beyond the physical and observable universe. After all, having faith is supernatural in itself. To never see God yet believe he's real. To never experience heaven yet believe it's waiting for us when we die. To never have witnessed the resurrection of Jesus yet believe it really happened. Faith is trusting the promises of God and believing what he says in his Word is true. If we can acknowledge these supernatural beliefs in the *light*, then why do we sometimes shy away from believing the *darkness*? Are we afraid that by bringing it up we will invite the darkness in? Do we think that if we ignore it completely it will just leave us alone?

Whatever the reason, downplaying the Enemy is dangerous. He's real, and his darkness plagues humanity. He wants to distract us, isolate us, scare us, and threaten us. He whispers questions that make us doubt.

Is this whole God thing even real?
Am I ever going to get better?

Wouldn't everyone just be better off without me?
Does God really care about me?
Do my friends really care about me?
What's the point of all this anyway?

When we rise up, when we chase after the light, the darkness will continue to bombard us. We may think that because we believe in Jesus, we are somehow immune to the Enemy's persecution, but that's not true. Rather, 1 Peter 5:8–9 reveals that "the Devil is poised to pounce, and would like nothing better than to catch you napping," and we must "keep a firm grip on the faith" (THE MESSAGE).

We're in a battle of good and evil, darkness and light, life and death. It's why news outlets stay in business; it's why there is never a lack of sad stories or world crises. This place we call home is broken. It's been broken and busted since the beginning, since that very first bite of the forbidden fruit. And the brokenness doesn't just tear us apart—it breaks God's heart. That's why he sent his one and only Son to save us forever. But God's story isn't over. We live in the meantime. He isn't finished writing his story or yours or mine. He knows how this all plays out, and we each get to play our part. That's why we must live with an awareness of the things we cannot see.

The Wilderness

Jesus knew all about this battle. Before his ministry even began, the Enemy tried to distract him from the calling God had placed on his life. We know that immediately after Jesus was baptized by John the Baptist, the Spirit led him into the wilderness to be tested. He prepared for the test by fasting for forty days and forty nights, and he was hungry. (I love how the Bible so clearly reminds us of Jesus' humanity: his hunger makes him human. If we fasted for forty days, we would be hungry too.) That's when we see the Enemy step into the ministry of Jesus for the first time. He said to Jesus, "Since you are God's Son, speak the word that will turn these stones into loaves of bread" (Matt. 4:3 THE MESSAGE).

Jesus responded, quoting Deuteronomy: "It takes more than bread to stay alive. It takes a steady stream of words from God's mouth" (v. 4).

Isn't it interesting how the Enemy approached Jesus with a question? Hasn't this always been his tactic? When he first stepped on the scene with Adam and Eve, in the place where perfect fell apart, he asked them, "Did God *really* say . . . ?" (Gen. 3:1, emphasis mine). This is what the Enemy does. He waits, he watches, and then he attacks. He *waited* forty days before he ever said anything to Jesus. He *watched* Jesus grow hungry and tired. Then he *attacked* Jesus right where his pain was the worst, taunting: "Since you are God's Son, speak the word that will turn these stones into loaves of bread."

How we respond to temptation determines our destination. If we lean into temptation, it will lead us to places we do not want to go. It will lead us away from the promises of God, away from the people we love the most, and away from our potential and our purpose. But how do we know whose voice we are listening to? How do we know if the still, small whisper is God or the Enemy?

I believe the distinction lies in the tone. The voice of God will never put us down. When we accept Jesus as our Lord and Savior and invite the Holy Spirit to dwell within us, we receive a new inner compass, new strong convictions, and a new everlasting encourager whose goal isn't to destroy but to edify. *Edify* comes from the Latin *aedes*, meaning "house" or "temple."[1] If our body is a temple—or house—then we are all fixer-uppers; we all need a master constructer who is willing to do a good work in us. None of us has arrived in this life; we are all a work in progress. Sometimes we need only a bathroom remodel; other times our walls need to be torn down and replaced with a new framework. But like any good HGTV show, the big reveal at the end, where we compare the before to the after, will shock and awe everyone, including us, as we look over the handiwork of the One who designed it all. God wants us to open the front door and invite him in to do the work. And guess what? He's already paid the price, so he's willing to work for free.

The Enemy, on the other hand, wants to tear the house down. He wants to take our fixer-upper and make it the worst house in the neighborhood. He wants to build new walls that completely surround the exterior so no one can get in. He wants to close the shutters, pull the drapes, and leave us locked up in the dark. His goal isn't to edify—it's to terrify. His voice is the voice of discouragement. It's the voice that says we aren't good enough, we aren't qualified, and we will never amount to anything. It's the voice that whispers, "You're ugly, you're unlovable, you're helpless, you're useless, your life is pointless." It's the voice of destruction, not instruction. It's the loud inner critic whose expectations are so high, we will never reach them.

While the Enemy sets the bar way too high, God goes low to sit beside us. I believe God's voice might sound like this: "There are no expectations; I love you just the way you are. You don't need to earn my love, you don't need to have it all together, you don't need to prove anything to me." He is the God of acceptance, not rejection. He would give up whole nations to save any one of our lives (Isa. 43:4). That's the kind of God we serve. He doesn't want to lead us astray; he wants to lead us in his way. He doesn't want to victimize, terrorize, or marginalize; instead he seeks to empathize, revise, and revolutionize our lives.

Another Encounter

The darkness continued to pursue Andrew relentlessly. He would often experience encounters with the darkness in his dreams, and this became magnified during his battle with depression and anxiety. Throughout our last summer together Andrew would often recount the terrifying dreams in detail to me. Each time his eyes would open wide, and as he spoke I could sense the fear in his voice and his eyes. There was a war raging inside his mind, and it wasn't just physical or chemical, it was also spiritual. It was a deadly combination of mental illness and spiritual warfare, and it was spiraling out of control.

But Andrew was determined to win. He was running to God,

clinging to the promises he knew to be true. Declaring "God's Got This," even in his weakest moments. His faith, though tired and weary, was still intact, and it gave me hope. Andrew wanted nothing more than to have his life back. He wanted to be back in the saddle, back in his sweet spot, back in his calling, back in the position he loved as lead pastor. So, with a green light from the doctors and the board of directors, we made a plan. After nearly four months of rest on the sabbatical, Andrew would return to work on August 1, 2018, and he would ease back into his responsibilities as lead pastor of our church. Andrew seemed excited and eager to lead again. He knew his comeback would be special, and he was planning to tackle the topic of mental illness head-on in a message series he titled "Hot Mess."

Just before his big return, Andrew had another encounter with the darkness, and this time it wasn't in his dreams. I was sitting on our front porch watching the boys play in our long driveway when my phone buzzed. It was a text from Andrew that read, "Five creatures surrounding me right now in my room. Each one has a meaning. Each one talking, taking turns. I'm praying them away. Might need some spiritual prayers to help. God is more powerful. God's got this. But I am scared in this moment."

I dropped my phone on the porch and ran through the house, down the long hallway, and back to our bedroom. I flung open the door, and there he was, the man I loved, absolutely paralyzed by fear. He was lying on the bed, he had the sheet pulled up over his head, and he was curled in a ball, trembling. I gently pulled back the covers, kissed his sweaty brow, and laid my hand on his chest.

"Babe, what's going on? Are you okay? I got your text. What can I do to help?" He didn't respond.

I looked around the room and didn't see any dark creatures; in my spirit I didn't feel any evil presence. So many thoughts swirled through my mind. *Is this all in his head? Is he experiencing some sort of hallucination? Is this really spiritual warfare?* I didn't have answers, but I knew I could do what I had always done since that very first encounter: pray.

I was in over my head in so many ways. All three of our boys came into our bedroom. They were beginning to jump on the bed. They missed their daddy; we all missed him. He spent countless hours alone in the bedroom, and it seemed like there wasn't anything we could do to make it better. I calmed the boys down, held them tight, asked each one to place their hands on their dad, and we prayed. We prayed hard. I was angry with God, I was angry with our circumstances, and I was confused. I hated the darkness. I hated these attacks. I hated the games the Enemy seemed to be playing in my husband's mind. I prayed hard, and I called reinforcements.

I called one of my best friends to pray for him, then I called and invited some members from our staff to come over to the house to pray. If this was spiritual warfare and the Enemy wasn't going to back down, I wasn't either. We couldn't live like this anymore.

The staff members arrived with anointing oil, and together we stopped and prayed over every room in our home. Then we circled Andrew, anointed him with oil, and each prayed for freedom and healing in his life. I wish I could say we saw miracles that day and

Andrew was healed on the spot, but he wasn't. The prayers of my friends, just like the prayers I had been praying all summer, seemed to fall flat. In my heart I cried out to God in desperation. I begged for breakthrough and healing in our home.

The Wilderness

Whenever I remember how lost and confused I felt in the wilderness of Andrew's fear, mental illness, and spiritual warfare, I can't help but think about Jesus as he, too, faced the Enemy in a wilderness. How did he respond? And did the Enemy just leave him alone? We know the Enemy waited, watched, and attacked him right where it hurt—in his hunger and pain—but then what?

> For the second test the Devil took him to the Holy City. He sat him on top of the Temple and said, "Since you are God's Son, jump." The Devil goaded him by quoting Psalm 91: "He has placed you in the care of angels. They will catch you so that you won't so much as stub your toe on a stone."
>
> Jesus countered with another citation from Deuteronomy: "Don't you dare test the Lord your God."
>
> For the third test, the Devil took him to the peak of a huge mountain. He gestured expansively, pointing out all the earth's kingdoms, how glorious they all were. Then he said, "They're yours—lock, stock, and barrel. Just go down on your knees and worship me, and they're yours."

Jesus' refusal was curt: "Beat it, Satan!" He backed his rebuke with a third quotation from Deuteronomy: "Worship the Lord your God, and only him. Serve him with absolute single-heartedness."

The Test was over. The Devil left. (Matt. 4:5–11 THE MESSAGE)

The Enemy didn't leave Jesus alone right away. It took three different interactions, three separate tests, before he left. Jesus, the Son of God, surely could have snapped his fingers and made the Enemy disappear in an instant, but he didn't. I don't know why he didn't, but I'm grateful he didn't because I think we can learn from Jesus how to respond in the face of our own trials. Instead of entertaining the ideas the Enemy was throwing his way, Jesus pulled wisdom from another wilderness story: the story of the Israelites wandering in the desert from the book of Deuteronomy.

I can see so much of my story in Jesus' temptation because the Enemy didn't back down for Andrew and me either. I've discovered that the Enemy is *relentless*. The Enemy will always try to find a way to invade our peace. Our greatest task as followers of Jesus is to understand the heart of God, a heart that is full of love and only love. Then we can know that fear, isolation, and despair are not from God. That despite the swirling, terrifying chaos of our broken world or minds, we have a calm, quiet place to dwell.

Even when Andrew was terrified and confused, he knew God's love was greater than his fear. He was still willing to declare, "God's got this." And I think that's really brave. To paraphrase author and adventurer Bear Grylls, perhaps being brave doesn't mean we are never afraid; perhaps being brave means being afraid but finding a way through it.

The Enemy wants us to feel isolated, unloved, and worthless. But the truth is this: every life matters, every story matters, and each and every one of us is loved and valued more than we could ever imagine. God wants to write a beautiful story through each of our lives. No matter who we are, no matter our past, no matter our mistakes, and no matter our mental health, he is with us, he is for us, and he is on our side.

SIX

Hot Mess

Despite the spiritual warfare, Andrew went back to work and courageously delivered two very powerful messages on mental illness in the Hot Mess series. He used his own experience to shine a bright light on a subject few pastors have the courage to touch. He had done his research, he knew the facts, he had memorized the statistics, and he even gave out the suicide hotline number and encouraged others to use it. He wasn't back to 100 percent yet; he was still healing. And he was very honest about where he was on the healing journey. He told our family and our church he was at about 65 percent capacity and was hoping to ease back into his responsibilities as lead pastor over time.

At home, behind the scenes, he was still struggling. One night he came into the kitchen and noticed I was feeling discouraged and sad. He asked, "What's wrong, Kayla?" He made eye contact with me from across the counter, his big blue eyes searching for some sense of connection with mine. He was wearing a white tank top and swim shorts, the same outfit he had worn nearly every day over the summer. The muscles in his shoulders and arms looked strong. The hours he had been spending lifting weights in the garage had clearly paid off. But it was just a façade. Despite his obvious external strength, there was an internal weakness he couldn't shake.

I heard his question, but I looked away before I said, "I'm just tired. I feel like I'm doing everything on my own. Our house feels like a war zone. The boys run around yelling and fighting all day, and I'm at my wit's end with it all. I can't keep up. I feel so alone."

When he didn't respond, I looked at him. He was tracing his fingers on the brown speckled granite. Then he said, "I'm sorry I haven't been there for you like you need me to be, like the boys need me to be. I was up again last night, in the middle of the night. I was standing right here in the kitchen. I had papers spread all over the counter, trying to come up with a new organization chart for the church and feeling really overwhelmed and confused. And I thought about killing myself."

My stomach sank. He was looking for compassion and connection, but I had nothing left to give. I was running on empty. I had told him I was tired and overwhelmed, and now he was telling me that he was just going to leave me?

"Andrew, you know that is the most selfish thing you could ever do, right? What about me? What about the boys? Andrew, you couldn't do that to the boys. They love you so much. How far did you think about it? Did you google it? Did you research how to do it? You wouldn't actually do that, right?" I was mad, confused, and stunned. He was being vulnerable and honest, and my mind wasn't in a healthy enough place to handle it.

"Kayla, that's not what you say to someone who is talking about suicide. You need to do some research and come up with something better to say. No, I didn't google it. No, I don't know how I would do it. It was just a moment. It was just a passing thought.

It was there and then it was gone. And then I put my papers away and went back to bed."

I wish I could say I got off my stool, walked around the kitchen island, and gave him a big hug. That I heard the utter despair in his voice and responded with compassion. But I didn't. I was upset. It felt like another blow, another thing added to my already overflowing plate. It was devastating to hear that he thought the solution to our problems was for him to die and leave me all alone to figure things out.

Worst of all, I didn't think he was serious. How could he be? He had everything he could ever want. He was at the top of his career, we'd just moved into a big, beautiful home. He had three boys who adored him, a wife who loved him deeply, a family who would drop anything and everything to be there for him, and a church who was cheering him on throughout his health journey. I didn't believe he would actually kill himself; I was so deeply convinced of this truth, I never brought it up again. That night at the kitchen counter was the one and only time Andrew ever mentioned suicide. This is a regret I will live with for the rest of my life.

I'm still asking myself, *Why didn't I take it seriously? Why didn't I seek to understand and empathize? Why did the word* suicide *erupt so many emotions inside of me? Why did I react instead of respond?*

It's difficult to know what to say when someone we love shares such a deep, dark thought with us. This was the first time in my life that someone close to me had ever talked about suicide. I was so ill-informed, so inexperienced, and so completely overwhelmed that I brushed it off. I didn't listen; I didn't sympathize. Instead I criticized. What I didn't understand is that when someone expresses thoughts of suicide, it's time to pay attention. It's time to ask questions, listen intently, and respond with a heart of love.

A Better Response

The word *suicide* has become a taboo in our society. Instead of talking about it openly and freely, it is something we keep private and tucked away. Why is there so much shame and fear surrounding suicide? And what can we do to change it?

We have to change the way we talk about it. There are too many good men and women, fathers and mothers, sons and daughters, coworkers and friends dying around us every single day. These are real people with seemingly beautiful lives who are silently struggling in the dark with agonizing thoughts of ending their pain forever.

The statistics don't lie. Suicide is a worldwide problem. Roughly 800,000 people die by suicide in the world every year. Broken down, that's one person every forty seconds.[1] In the United States alone, suicide is the second leading cause of death among individuals between the ages of ten and thirty-four.[2] In 2017 there were more than twice as many suicides in the United States as there were homicides.[3] We have to find a way to save more lives. If people are brave enough to share their darkest thoughts, the best thing we can do is respond, not react. Here are a few ways to do that.

LISTEN

Let them talk! Let them vent. It's good they feel safe enough to talk about it. Lean in, be fully present in the moment, ask questions, and talk less.

OFFER EMPATHY

Instead of being shocked or angry, remain calm. Let them know their feelings are valid, tell them how important they are, and remind them this is not the end and help is available. Don't use the word *selfish* like I did. Although it may appear that way, *suicide isn't selfish.* Those suffering from suicidal ideation genuinely believe everyone would be better off without them; they believe their death is the solution to their pain. Labeling them as selfish only heaps more pain onto their already broken minds.

TAKE IT SERIOUSLY

Any talk of suicide should be taken seriously. Follow up and ask questions like:

"Do you have a suicide plan?"
"Do you know when or how you would do it?"
"How often do you think about it?"
"What problem are you trying to solve through suicide?"

These questions can help lessen pain and can lead to unexplored solutions.

REACH OUT FOR HELP

We must do everything in our power to get them the help they need. Call a crisis line for advice (suicide hotline number: 1–800-273-8255), encourage them to seek professional help, and find a way to ensure that a friend or family member goes with them to every doctor's appointment.

KEEP SHOWING UP

Don't just say, "Call me if you need anything." Be love in action. Show up at the front door. Keep calling until they answer. Invite them, include them, and continue to reach out until they get better.

When we shut down someone who is struggling with suicidal thoughts, the chances of the conversation surfacing again are slim to none. If we aren't careful, we may miss the one and only opportunity to save a life. Typically, our first reaction is not our best response. If you are taken by surprise like I was, take a moment to pause and remember those four powerful words: "I have no idea."

The Unimaginable

We believed Andrew was improving. Our family, our staff, and the medical professionals all thought he had turned the corner, but during Andrew's third week back to work, everything changed.

Andrew was having a good week. He was full of anticipation for the message he was planning to deliver on Sunday. He was also gearing up for a big team rally on Friday night, something our church called "team night." It was a full week, but he was excited about what God was going to do in and through him. I knew he was excited because he expressed it through our conversations and even on social media. On Wednesday morning he posted a video to his Instagram story from his home office. It was a peaceful morning. The sun was shining, his window was cracked open, and a slight breeze was blowing through the trees. Our small front-yard waterfall was trickling. He wrote, "Can't complain about the sounds and views from my home study."

However, by Wednesday night, fear and anxiety began to cloud his mind again. The boys were asleep, and we were sitting on our zero-gravity chairs in the backyard. Andrew had his computer open and was working on his talk for team night. He was feeling anxious about it and wasn't sure if he would have the capacity to deliver two separate messages that week, one on team night and a different one on Sunday. Like we did for most of his messages, we sat in the backyard and worked it out. He talked, I listened, and we came up with solutions together. I loved *together*. I loved what we were building. I loved being his wife. Leading the church with him was and still is one of the greatest honors of my life. I found value and purpose in supporting the call God had placed on my guy. His calling became my calling.

However, it wasn't always easy. Being at the top of any organization isn't always easy. It's true what they say: it's lonely at the top. Harsh, hurtful emails find their way into inboxes at the top. Leaders are easy to blame for things that go wrong, and at the end of the day, the top dogs are responsible for the success or failure of a business. Andrew would often refer to himself as the "linchpin," the one holding everything in place, and in some ways he was. He had done everything he could to hold the church together through his dad's leukemia journey. Now he was grappling to hold the church together through his own mental illness journey, but it was slowly slipping through his fingers.

After we worked through the fear and anxiety surrounding his messages that week, we went back to our bedroom to pray. We lay on the bed, he gently rested his head on my lap, and I ran my fingers through his coarse brown hair as I'd done countless times before. Then I prayed. I could tell his mind was still sick, that he was pushing through confusing fear and pain. Everything in him desperately wanted to be better, desperately wanted to be back to 100 percent. It frustrated him immensely that this was slowing him down. We all wanted freedom from his mental health complications, but freedom always felt out of reach.

When I finished praying, Andrew immediately stood up and walked outside. He seemed frustrated all over again, and it broke my heart. I'd hoped praying together would help him relax and lead him back to peace, but it didn't. All my efforts to help, no matter how pure, sweet, and nurturing, couldn't touch the war raging inside his mind. As he was pacing around the backyard, I remember saying out loud, "God, why is he so unhappy?"

The next day I woke up early, like I did most mornings, to spend some quiet time alone. This is the prayer I scribbled in my journal before anyone woke up, before our lives changed forever:

God, thank you for another day. Thank you for helping me have a better, healthier, fresh perspective on life, my husband, and our boys. Thank you for helping me discern what to say or not to say. Thank you for giving me joy for my kids and peace. I pray over these next few days. I pray that Andrew's meetings today would go really well. That he would be calm, that he would be strong, that he would connect well. Please help him to weather all of this well and to grow out of the pit he is in. I miss my husband. I miss the Andrew he was before all of this. I pray he would have newfound hope, newfound joy, newfound peace, and that he would run to you. I pray that the right people would come to the team out of nowhere. I pray that he would be able to organize the staff well, so it best supports him.

God, thank you for giving me the energy and compassion I need to be supportive. Please continue to fill me up so that I can continue to pour out every day. Please continue to give me wisdom; thank you for growing me in so many ways, for stretching me beyond my limits, and for walking beside me through the fire. God, I cling to you, your hope, your words. Please lead my mind, my heart, my spirit, and my soul. Please help me to love others well today and be a light for you. I love you, God, amen.

Hope is what I had.
Hope we would one day find solid ground again.
Hope this was just a temporary darkness.
Hope healing was waiting for us off in the distance.
Hope Andrew would rediscover himself.

Hope this was just the beginning of our lives, not the end.

A few hours later, Andrew called me, and he was in the middle of what I can only describe as an "episode." He had received some unsettling information during a meeting at the office, which his broken mind couldn't process rationally. His healthy mind would have been able to shake it off, come up with solutions, and move on with the day. But he wasn't healthy; he was still sick. With the help of our immediate family, we were able to move Andrew to a quiet, safe location. We surrounded him with love, care, and empathy. We listened to him talk for hours as he processed his pain out loud.

As Andrew continued to process his emotions, anger grew inside of him. We tried to better understand where the anger was stemming from, but all Andrew could say was, "Anger is fear!" I didn't understand what he meant by *fear*. I didn't know where the fear was coming from, and I didn't know how to help him. I had been living with the extremes of his mental illness all summer. I was tired, and I reached my own breaking point. I excused myself from the situation and drove home crying. I needed to pause. I needed to clear my mind so that I could better respond to Andrew from a place of love instead of exhaustion and pain.

I drove home alone, and I didn't call anyone. To be honest, I still felt like I couldn't call anyone. I felt confused and very far from the hope I'd had in the quiet calm of the morning. Hope for a good day, hope for a better life, hope for healing—it all seemed a million miles away.

The next morning, I dropped my oldest son, Smith, off at kindergarten, stopped by a local donut shop to grab breakfast for my other two boys, and then went to meet with a few immediate family members to discuss the next steps to take for Andrew's health. As a family, we had worked through his health complications before, and I was confident this was just another hurdle; we would find a way to move forward from this too. As we made phone calls and scheduled meetings, the unimaginable took place. Andrew, who had been left alone to rest, attempted suicide.

As I arrived on the scene, I began screaming, yelling, asking over and over again, "Is he dead? Is he going to be okay? What happened?"

I was out of my mind, out of my body. In complete panic, I cried, moaned, wailed. I made sounds I didn't even know I could make, and I pounded on the floor. I was in disbelief. After what felt like hours, the paramedics were able to find a pulse. They loaded Andrew into an ambulance and took him to the hospital. I followed in a car close behind. My mind was spinning out of control, tears were streaming down my face, and I was deeply confused. The husband I loved and adored, the father of our beautiful boys, the pastor of our incredible church—this could not be happening to him.

I prayed the same prayer over and over again during the twenty-minute drive to the hospital. "God, we need a miracle. God, please." I deeply believed God would save him, God would pull him through, God wouldn't allow another tragedy to hit our family and our church. This wouldn't be the end of Andrew's life.

I arrived at the hospital and waited in a cold, small room with another family member and a member from our staff. After the doctors ran necessary tests and hooked his fragile body up to numerous machines, they gave us the green light to enter his room. I ran in, flung my body onto his, and wept. Through my tears I whispered over and over again, "I'm so sorry." My heart was shattered. Guilt weighed heavily on my body and my soul. I felt like I should have done more, like I could have prevented this from happening, like it was all my fault. The man I loved, the man whose head I'd cradled in my lap just a few nights before, the man I'd built my life with, the man I'd made a family with, the man I had hoped to grow old with was just inches away from death. How could this be happening?

This is suicide.

The blindside we hate. It's unpredictable, irrational, and tragic. Our finite minds have no place to categorize it. We weren't created to process this kind of pain and death. Sadly, my story is one many have lived or will live. In the wake of my husband's suicide, I've learned there are many painful misconceptions about this type of tragedy, and we need to do better. We need to change the way we approach and talk about suicide. By seeking to understand and empathize, we will begin to break the stigma and can come alongside those who are struggling—those who are experiencing suicidal thoughts or those who have lost a loved one to suicide.

Myth #1: Suicide is an unforgivable sin.

This is a common misconception that's been debated in religious circles for centuries. The theological framework for it was first introduced through the bishop Saint Augustine in his book *The City of God.* In the book, Augustine states several arguments against suicide, claiming that those who take their life into their own hands look away from God and commit murder. He justified this through his interpretation of the commandment "Thou shalt not kill" (Ex. 20:13 KJV). He considered suicide an unforgivable sin—a murder of self that allowed no room for repentance.[4]

As this philosophy spread, suicide became regarded as a sinful crime. People who died by suicide were punished and even denied a Christian burial. Attempted suicides also had harsh consequences that could lead to punishment by excommunication. It wasn't until the 1990s that the Catholic Church began to see suicide differently, and for the first time the catechism of the Catholic Church acknowledged, "Grave psychological disturbances, anguish, or grave fear of hardship, suffering, or torture can diminish the responsibility of the one committing suicide. We should not despair of the eternal salvation of persons who have taken their own lives. By ways known to him alone, God can provide the opportunity for . . . repentance."[5]

I'll be the first to admit that prior to Andrew's suicide, I may have actually believed the words of Saint Augustine. I remember leaning over to my mother-in-law, Carol, in the hospital room and whispering through my tears, "Will he go to heaven?" She quickly reassured me, and I am confident now: our acceptance into eternity doesn't hinge on how we die; instead it hinges on our salvation, our personal relationship with Jesus. I was relieved by her response and now confidently believe this to be true. Although Andrew's life was cut short—and I truly believe suicide was not God's plan for his life—I can rest knowing his salvation is secure and he is at peace in eternity.

Myth #2: Suicide is selfish.

The ripple effect of suicide is terribly destructive, but can suicide really be considered selfish? The main question I received after Andrew's suicide was, "How could he do that to his family?" It's a question I ask myself all the time because the Andrew I knew would never have wanted to cause me, the boys, our family, or our church pain. The Andrew I knew loved his life. He looked to the future and saw hope, not doom. There's only one appropriate answer to this question that I can reconcile in my mind: *it wasn't him*. His mind was sick, and I will never fully grasp or understand what those final moments leading up to the suicide were like for him.

As I have wrestled with this notion, I have also done research. The truth, I have found, is that the suicidal mind is in an altered state of consciousness, which causes significantly distorted thinking.[6] Reality becomes blurred as the mind fixates on the idea that the suffering individual is a burden and won't be missed. These toxic thoughts lead to isolation, and soon suicide seems like the only solution to escape unbearable pain.

Self-proclaimed "suicidologist" Edwin Shneidman coined the term *psychache* to describe this kind of unbearable psychological pain. In his book *Autopsy of a Suicidal Mind*, Shneidman described psychache as a pain that darkens life. A pain that is "unbearable, intolerable, unendurable, and unacceptable." And in this type of pain, it becomes better to "stop the cacophony" than to endure the noise.[7] Shneidman theorized that unresolved psychache results in suicidal behavior. Through his extensive research he discovered psychache to be the cause in nearly every case of suicide.

Andrew's mind was broken, and he was in pain. I can't even begin to wrap my mind around what those moments must have felt like. Imagine the torment and torture it must take for any human being to go against the human will to survive and ultimately die by suicide. Although there are times when I feel angry at Andrew, and although I still have questions he will never be able to answer, I do not blame him for his death. He was sick, his mind was overcome with pain, and his death is a tragedy.

Myth #3: If you truly believe in God you will never have suicidal thoughts.

Andrew loved God and ran to him in his depression. He filled his alone time with worship music. He spent time reading Scripture and sitting with God in prayer. He leaned into his faith to carry him through some of his darkest moments. Just like Andrew, we see heroes of our faith struggle with the darkness of their minds all throughout Scripture:

- David wrote in a psalm, "How long, LORD? Will you forget me forever? How long will you hide your face from me? How long must I wrestle with my thoughts and day after day have sorrow in my heart? How long will my enemy triumph over me?" (Ps. 13:1–2)

- Jonah in his anger with God prayed, "LORD, please take my life from me, for it is better for me to die than to live!" (Jonah 4:3 NKJV)
- Moses, in his feelings of disappointment and betrayal by his own people, cried out, "But now, please forgive their sin—but if not, then blot me out of the book you have written." (Ex. 32:32)
- Jesus in the garden of Gethsemane, overcome with anguish, declared, "My soul is overwhelmed with sorrow to the point of death." (Matt. 26:38)

The difficulty of life sometimes takes a devastating toll on our minds. Although we serve a God of miracles who is powerful enough to rescue anyone from the grips of depression or suicidal ideation, the truth is sometimes he doesn't. Sometimes those who are suffering feel much like David and are asking God, "How long must I wrestle with my thoughts and day after day have sorrow in my heart?"

The Wilderness

Even our darkest thoughts will never separate us from the love of God. He is with us in the wilderness, and he is with us as we wrestle with our brokenness. He is with us as we ask the hard questions from our places of pain. He is with us as we fight to make it through each day. If you are silently struggling with suicidal thoughts and you are thinking about leaving for good, please fight to stay. I know your overwhelming pain is real. I have wrestled with thoughts of leaving this place and my pain forever too. But learning to live with the pain is possible. And building a beautiful life around the pain is possible too. To stay is a brave choice, maybe the bravest choice you will ever make. And if you can't choose it for yourself, then please look around and choose to stay for the ones you love. They need you, we need you, and we don't want to stay here without you.

Continue to wrestle, continue to fight, continue to push through one more minute, one more hour, one more day. Let the breath in your lungs be a reminder of the grace that covers everything. It covers the darkness, it covers anxiety, it covers depression, and it covers suicidal ideation. His grace is how we all make it through another day. We are all broken people, we all carry pain, and we are all covered in the light of his mighty love. A light that is strong enough to pierce through every dark, confusing, and isolating place. A light that offers real, true hope—a lifeline light that reaches through our pain and leads us back to peace. You may feel completely surrounded by darkness, but I promise you, friend, if you look hard enough, you will find a glimmer of light, and maybe a glimmer is enough for today. You are not alone. You are loved. Your life matters.

SEVEN

Goodbye to Everything

Our family was familiar with hospitals, nurses, and beeping machines. We had lived in and out of the hospital for four years while Andrew's dad fought for his life against unrelenting leukemia. It had been three years since David lost his fight and entered eternity, and now Andrew? It didn't feel real; it couldn't be real. How could this be happening again? How had we ended up in another hospital room, surrounding another man we loved?

Shock paralyzed my entire body. My head was spinning, my stomach was in knots, and my chest felt tight and heavy. Everything was blurry as I lay on the small hospital bed holding my husband. All I could do was pray. I prayed the same prayer I had prayed on the way to the hospital: "God, we need a miracle. God, please." I kept begging for supernatural intervention, begging God to write a different ending, begging God to step in and perform a miracle, one only he could do. We waited hours for results from the doctor. Results that would tell us if Andrew would live or die.

How do you wait for something like that? How do you process death by suicide? How do you say goodbye? I held on to hope like I held on to Andrew, gripping as tightly as I could. Surely, I reasoned, God wouldn't allow this to happen to our family again—would he?

The machines were keeping Andrew alive, but Andrew wasn't

there. I wondered where he was. *Is he already in heaven with his dad? Will he come back to be with us? Is this the end?* Thoughts bounced off every corner of my mind, and the same two words remained on my tongue. "God, please."

Out of desperation I posted a picture to Instagram begging everyone we knew to pray. The caption read, "Friends, we need your prayer! Please pray for complete healing for this man. He is in the hospital on life support after attempting to take his own life this morning. We need a miracle. Please pray."[1]

I truly believed that with enough prayer, Andrew would live. We were at war with mortality. We were at war with the Enemy. We were at war with time. How much would he have left? I wanted to reverse it all; I wanted to turn back the clock and save him. Yet I knew all of the rescue scenarios playing through my mind would never work. There was no way to turn back time. All we could do was wait.

Word spread about Andrew's attempted suicide, and everyone we knew, along with thousands of people we didn't know, was praying. Waiting and praying, praying and waiting, for hours. Finally, the doctor entered the room to share the test results. His report was quick—just another day on the job for the young doctor. Without an ounce of emotion or empathy, he explained that Andrew's body had been damaged beyond repair. Our heads fell into our hands and we wept. The sounds emerging from the depths of our souls filled that cold hospital room. Beeping machines and cries of broken, shattered hearts.

I didn't want to say goodbye; I didn't want to believe any of this was real. I was angry at God, asking him, "How could you? Why did you allow this to happen? Why Andrew?"

Our room was full of weeping and worship; it was all we could do. We stood around his bedside and read Psalm 23.

The LORD is my shepherd, I lack nothing. He makes me lie down in green pastures, he leads me beside quiet waters, he refreshes my soul. He guides me along the right paths for his name's sake. Even though I walk through the darkest valley, I will fear no evil, for you are with me; your rod and your staff, they comfort me.

You prepare a table before me in the presence of my enemies. You anoint my head with oil; my cup overflows. Surely your goodness and love will follow me all the days of my life, and I will dwell in the house of the LORD forever.

I wanted time to lie next to him and hold his warm body for as long as possible. Thankfully God gave us the gift of one last day, but we knew heaven was quickly calling Andrew home. We surrounded Andrew with our love. We played his favorite songs, we cried, we talked, we prayed, and we kept holding out for a miracle. "If only you could wake him up, God. Imagine the testimony he could tell. Imagine how many lives he could impact for you. Imagine how many lives could be saved through his story. God, his boys need him; our church needs him; I need him. God, please."

Then, just as quickly as the nightmare had started, it was over. With one last breath, he was gone. I lay on the small hospital bed one more time, and I screamed, cried, yelled. And then I said goodbye.

Goodbye to everything.

Goodbye to the love of my life.

Goodbye to growing old together.

Goodbye to life as I knew it.

Goodbye to every dream I ever had.

Goodbye to my best friend.

Goodbye to parenting together.

Goodbye to my beautiful life.

Goodbye to love.

I walked down the hallway to a waiting room full of close friends and family and whispered, "He's gone." We held each other and wept in utter disbelief. After a while, someone went to get the car to take us home, and as it pulled into the circle drive, I fell to my knees. It was Andrew's car, the car he loved to drive as fast as he could down the last long road that led to our home, the car we took on road trips together, just the two of us. I could hardly pull myself off the ground and into the car; the pain was overwhelming.

The day Andrew died will forever be etched into my mind: August 25, 2018, the darkest day of my life. The day *everything* changed. The day my old life died and a different, unwanted life began. This new life terrified me to my core. It was a life I didn't want to live alone, a life I hadn't signed up for. I wanted my old life back. I wanted my guy back. I wanted to wake up from this horrific nightmare.

The next morning, the news of Andrew's passing was announced at our church, and I made my own announcement on Instagram to update my friends who were praying and to protect and honor my guy. Suicide wouldn't get the last word.

Last night, the love of my life, the father of my children, and the pastor of our incredible church took his last breath and went to be with Jesus. It wasn't the miracle I was hoping for, but he is now in heaven with his dad, free of pain, free of depression and anxiety.

He was an amazing husband. He truly made me better, made me feel like the most beautiful girl in the world, and he loved me so deeply. We fit so well together; we were one. He was an amazing daddy; his three boys are going to miss him so much. He had such a unique and special relationship with each of them. He was an incredibly gifted teacher, communicator, and pastor. He was special, one of a kind, and will be missed by thousands of people all around the world.

Please pray for me and the boys. I don't know how I am going to face this. I am completely heartbroken, lost, and empty. Never in a million years would I have imagined this would be the end of his story.

If you are struggling with suicidal thoughts or actions, please tell someone. Please make sure you're not alone, and please call a friend or family member before you make that irreversible decision. You are loved and valued more than you know! #godsgotthis[2]

As I look back on the words I shared that day, there is one word that stands out boldly to me: *decision*. It's a word I have been grappling with since the day of Andrew's suicide. I have a very difficult time believing his suicide was a decision, and I would rather categorize it as a tragic accident.

I have determined that the words *decision* and *committed* are actually the wrong words to attach to suicide. The words *committed suicide* heap shame and blame onto the shoulders of the person who died. The word *committed* is one we attach to phrases like "committed a sin" or "committed murder" or "committed a crime." It ignores the fact that suicide is often the result of underlying mental illness. If someone had a heart condition and experienced a heart attack, we wouldn't say that person "committed a heart attack." Dying by suicide is the same, and I believe *died by suicide* is the best phrase to use. It clearly sends the message that the death was caused by a mental condition, not a decision.

This change in language might seem small or insignificant, but it's not. Our words matter. Our words carry weight; our words have consequences. Our words have the power to speak life or evoke pain and shame over someone. When we pay attention to the words we use to describe mental health issues, we fling the door wide open for our loved ones to finally feel brave enough to speak up, step out, raise their hands, and say, "I need help." If we want to save lives and break the stigma, we have to choose our words wisely. Our words should reflect the truth that people matter; they matter to God, and they matter to us. Every single life is valuable, and every single life is worth fighting for.

As our story continued to spread like wildfire, I continued to choose my words carefully. Our story and family photos were all over the news, and I suddenly had thousands of strangers following along on social media. I was shocked and never would have expected people from around the world to be praying for our family, sending letters of encouragement, and flooding our inboxes with messages of kindness and support. These were beautiful gifts to our shattered hearts, and we received them with open arms and gratitude.

Because Andrew had died by suicide, I knew that some people in the "big C" church community would look down on his death with judgment and criticism. I expected to receive harsh responses, but I was surprised to find the opposite from many Christians. Andrew's death seemed to have cracked open the door for a conversation the Church didn't know it needed to have, a conversation much bigger than I ever thought possible, all because our family was willing to say the word *suicide*. We weren't trying to hide the way that Andrew died. We knew it wasn't his fault, we knew it wasn't an "unforgivable sin" or "selfish act," and we wanted to prevent it from happening to other people. And it has done that. These are just a few of the thousands of messages that flooded my inbox the first week:

I finally reached out and started to get help, and I owe that a lot to you and your family for walking through this with such transparency, resilience, and grace. For the first time in my entire life I believe that I am going to beat this, and I owe it to Pastor Andrew and you. I am so sorry that you are walking through this, but I just wanted you to know that lives are being changed and people, like me, are choosing to live as a result.

It just never "clicked" in my head that I have purpose and [a] reason that Jesus put me on this earth. Until reading your post today. It was the first time someone from the outside of my family has spoken truth that it's OKAY to struggle. And it doesn't mean I am broken or not going to heaven or am alone. Sorry for the rambling but your post saved my life. And I felt like you needed to know that. Thank you for being a light to those who need it.

I know you don't have time or energy to respond to all the messages, but your story is the reason I called my husband's therapist and told her how bad it really was. Thank you.

While this won't change the pain and grief you feel, I wanted to tell you God has been working through this—your public grief has saved my life. I was contemplating suicide as I've battled a silent battle with anxiety and depression, and then I stumbled across the first blog post you wrote. Andrew's legacy lives on. I'm alive because of him. Now every dark night, I repeat to myself "God's got this! God is always enough!" Thank you.

Thank you for choosing to share your story! Because of it my husband and I have decided to continue our therapy. My husband's depression and shame had led to suicidal thoughts. He is also a pastor. God is using you . . . and I am praying you feel God's loving presence.

From a mom with a son who is seeking treatment for suicidal thoughts: thank you for sharing your life, your pain, and your journey. It has helped me help my son.

I wanted you to know you are making a difference. Your post encouraged me to check in with both of my adult daughters that struggle with mental health but always say, "It's no big deal, I can handle it." Thank you for your words and encouragement to keep asking.

I want you to know you have helped me so much. I've been grieving the loss of myself. Knowing I didn't want to be here anymore but also knowing I have a family I love too much. So I opened up to my husband last night and we are looking into therapists and resources for me. I guarantee that your beautiful posts have affected others this way and I can't thank you enough.

Every single letter of encouragement made me want to share my grief, my pain, and the things I was learning more. God was planting a burning message inside my heart. After just three days I wrote the first of a series of letters to Andrew. We posted the letter to our family blog, *God's Got This.*

To My Andrew,

It's only been 3 days. Nothing can take away the suffocating pain I feel now that you are gone. I miss every part of you, I see you everywhere. I replay the events of that fateful day over and over again in my mind wishing I could have done things differently. Wishing I could have held your hand one more time and prayed over you and told you how much I love you, how much I believe in you, and how God's got this too.

You were right all along; I truly didn't understand the depths of your depression and anxiety. I didn't understand how real and how relentless the spiritual attacks were. The pain, the fear, and the turmoil you must have been dealing with every single day is unimaginable. The enemy knew what an amazing man you were. The enemy knew God had huge plans for your life. The enemy saw how God was using your gifts, abilities, and unique teaching style to reach thousands of lives for Him. The enemy hated it and he pursued you incessantly. Taunting you and torturing you in ways that you were unable to express to anyone.

Andrew, I want to tell you from the depths of my heart and my pain that I am so sorry.

I am so sorry you were so scared.

I am so sorry you felt so alone.

I am so sorry you felt misunderstood.

I am so sorry you felt betrayed and deeply hurt by the words and actions of others.

I am so sorry you were fighting a dark, spiritual war virtually alone.

I am so sorry you were unable to fully get the help and support you needed.

I wish I had one more chance to hold you and cry with you and encourage you. I wish you could see the outpouring of love from people all over the world who have been impacted by your story. I wish you could hold your boys one more time and tell them goodbye. I wish we could go on one more trip together, just the two of us. I am not ready to say goodbye. I am so madly and deeply in love with you. Every part of me longs to be with you. I can't eat, I can't sleep, I can't function, and I feel so lost without you. You were my life. I was so proud to be your wife, Andrew. I was so proud to sit in the front row and watch you in your sweet spot on stage. I was always so amazed by you, every single day. You could do anything you set your mind to! You were handy, you made every home we lived in look beautiful inside and out. You were creative, you were funny, you were thoughtful, you were passionate, you had vision, you had charisma, and you were so special. You are irreplaceable, Andrew. There will never be another man like you.

I want to tell you that I am never going to stop fighting for you. I will continue to tell our community and our world what an amazing man you were. Your name will be honored, and you will be remembered as a hero. You fought the good fight, and I can only imagine the incredible place God had prepared for you when you walked through the gates of heaven. I can only imagine what it must have felt like to see your dad again, healthy and strong. I can only imagine how much joy you must feel now that you are truly free. I wish I could be there with you, celebrating on the streets of gold. But for now, I will continue to live for you. I will raise our boys to be men of God, just like you were. Your name will live on in a powerful way. Your story has the power to save lives, change lives, and transform the way the Church supports pastors.

I love you so much and I will miss you every single day for

the rest of my life. When I think of you I will smile, knowing that I will see you again one day. Thank you for 10 wonderful years together. Thank you for giving me the gift of three beautiful blue-eyed boys who all resemble you. Thank you for choosing me, for believing in me, and for showing me how to live fearlessly.

Until we meet again, I will cling to my Father in heaven. He will carry me through every second, every minute, every hour of every day. I read a verse this morning and I know God is reminding me that even now, in the midst of my deepest pain, He has got this.

"Because you are close to me and always available, my confidence will never be shaken, for I experience your wrap-around presence every moment" [(Ps. 16:8 TPT).]

With all my heart and all my love,
Your Girl[3]

Compassion isn't always the first response to suicide, but it should be. We will never fully understand the mystery of a suicidal mind. Unless we have experienced it ourselves, we will never fully know the depth of anguish that leads to suicide. Suicide is a tragedy, and no one is to blame. We cannot blame ourselves, we cannot blame others, and we cannot even place blame on our loved one who died. It has been said before, "Suicide is a permanent solution to a temporary problem." Maybe those we've lost to suicide truly believed their pain would never end and death was the only doorway to peace. I will never know what those final moments were like for Andrew, but I deeply believe his death wasn't his fault.

After I lost Andrew, I sat with close family and friends among the shrapnel of an explosion we never saw coming. We also sat with God. The presence of God filled every space of the home as I huddled with safe people to process the pain. When I cried until I couldn't cry anymore, God caught my tears. When I wondered how I would get through another day, God made a way. When I worried about what the future might look like, God continued working on my behalf to craft a beautiful redemption plan.

The Wilderness

As I think back to the story of Jesus in the wilderness, when he was worn out and weary after fasting for forty days and standing up to attacks from the Enemy, I see God sitting with him too. God didn't leave him alone in his pain and exhaustion; instead the Scripture says that God sent angels to comfort him. "The Test was over. The Devil left. And in his place, angels! Angels came and took care of Jesus' needs" (Matt. 4:11 THE MESSAGE). This is what God does. He holds us, he comforts us, and he sustains us when we have nothing left. "The LORD is close to the brokenhearted; he rescues those whose spirits are crushed" (Ps. 34:18 NLT).

God wants nothing more than to be close to us in our pain. I'll never forget Andrew's last message from the stage, less than a week before he died, titled "Mess to Masterpiece." He talked about how "mess" is the thing we all have in common. We are all a mess, none of us have it figured out, all of us are broken, and all of us fall short. It's the mess that brings us together and draws God near. If we weren't all a mess, we wouldn't need God.

Near the end of his message Andrew posed a question. "What is it in your mess or in your season that God is trying to do in you?"[4] It's a beautiful question, isn't it? When we ask this question from the depths of our pain, we can be rescued from a victim mentality and instead be motivated to take the next step toward healing. It's a question that can change the game, change the outcome, change our lives forever—if we let it. The truth is, God always has a rescue plan. There isn't a single situation or circumstance that's too messy for him. When we feel like everything has fallen apart and our life is in disarray, we can stop and say, "What is God trying to do in me?"

Despite our mess he calls us his masterpiece. "For we are God's masterpiece. He has created us anew in Christ Jesus, so we can do the good things he planned for us long ago." (Eph. 2:10 NLT). The word *masterpiece* comes from the Greek word *poiema*, from which we get the word *poem*. Just like a poem ebbs and flows, has ups and downs and highs and lows, so do we. From the moment we are born until the moment we take our last breath, we are God's instruments, his poiema. He is the master artist. He sets the scene, he writes the ballad, he decides the tone, and he determines the depth and breadth of its entirety. It's all up to him. When we realize control is just an illusion, we can let go, sit back, and let the master artist do his best work. We can allow him to write the script of becoming. We don't become who we want to become on our own. We only become someone when we realize it was never about us in the first place.

Before Andrew wrapped up that message, the very last one he would ever preach, he gave a challenge and a prayer. The challenge was this, "Tune in to what God is already trying to do in you."[5] We are all becoming. We are all poiema. We are all a work in progress. We are all a masterpiece in the making. We have all sinned, fallen short, and need a savior. Recognizing our need for him, we can surrender and step into his mighty rescue plan. He invites us to follow him in the middle of our mess, and he promises to lead us from the darkest of circumstances into the light. "I am the light of the world. Whoever follows me will never walk in darkness, but will have the light of life" (John 8:12).

As we tune in to what God is already trying to do, the next step is to surrender through prayer. The prayer Andrew prayed that day was simple: "Heavenly Father, complete the work you've begun in me."[6] It doesn't have to be complicated. It's simply recognizing that he is the artist, and we are the instruments. The masterpiece he is creating through each of our lives is unique, profound, deep, challenging, and beautiful.

As I sat with the overwhelming pain of Andrew's tragic death, I chose surrender. I was in over my head, drowning in a mess way too big for my mind to comprehend. I needed God more than I'd ever needed him before. I didn't want to be anywhere but close to him. Even in those dark, bleak moments, I felt a stirring in my soul. God, the master artist, the author of my poiema, was already working on the next line, the next rhyme, a new ballad to come. My life, his masterpiece, wasn't finished yet.

EIGHT

One Plot or Two

To my Andrew,

Today marks one week since that tragic morning. The darkest week of my life. The emotions that I have faced this week have crushed me: mind, body, and soul. The gaping hole I feel inside now that you are gone is suffocating. Oh, how I long to be with you right now. I would give anything just to cuddle up into your chest and hold you again.

The last few days have been incredibly difficult. There are countless decisions that need to be made to honor you and put your body to rest. What will you wear? What type of casket will you lie in? How will we pay for it? What location will be best? Do we buy 1 plot or 2? Who will speak at the service? These are questions we shouldn't be facing. These are questions I was supposed to answer 50 years from now when I am old and grey. How do I do this without you? Why are you gone so soon? How do I tell the boys?

Today we walked the cemetery. It was surreal. Overwhelming and peaceful at the same time. We felt a small kiss from God when He graciously provided a place for you right next to your dad. Now every time we visit, we can remember you both and imagine the joy you must feel now you are together.

Tomorrow I will tell the boys. The life they once knew will never be the same. The dreams they had with you are gone, just like mine. The daily routines, the daddy dates, the donut runs and the soccer games now distinctly different than before. The house will be quieter, lonelier, and duller without you. You filled our house with joy. You filled our home with fun and laughter that only comes from a dad. You knew how to crack just the right joke to cheer me up when life felt overwhelming. I miss you so much, Andrew, every single part.

I hate the loss and the pain, but there is nothing I can do to change it. There is nothing I can do to bring you back, so I will choose to lean [on] God. The stories flooding in are lifting me up and holding me up. The life change that is happening only comes from God because He promises to work all things together for good, even this.

Your story, your life and your death, is opening the door for conversations all around the world. Your story is helping people to share their hidden thoughts and secret struggles with their family and friends. Your story is paving the way for an even bigger conversation about how the church can better come alongside people with mental illness, including pastors. God is using your story and this tragedy to do miracles in the lives of other people. As much as I don't want to, I can't help but see God's hand in all of this.

My mind keeps wandering back to the last message you gave, titled "Mess to Masterpiece." Just as you told the church about how God will meet them in their mess, I believe God is meeting us, right here, right now, in this mess. And my prayer today in my darkest hour is, "Heavenly Father, complete the work you've begun in me." Only God can turn the greatest tragedy in my life into triumph.

> I love you and I miss you with
> every piece of me,
> Your Girl[1]

I sat cold and numb in a small office at the private, tree-lined cemetery. I'd heard the words, but my mind couldn't process them. "One plot or two?" Faced with a decision beyond the realm of possibility, I cried. *How am I supposed to continue living when the love of my life is gone?*

"You're young," the cemetery manager said. I was twenty-nine years old and picking out a plot for my husband. My beautiful husband who was so full of life. My husband who, as he lay dying in the hospital, still looked perfect to me. I needed to escape the moment; it was too much for my brain to process, for my heart to handle, and for my mind to comprehend. So I closed my eyes and went back to the hospital room, to the last time I felt his warmth.

From the top of his head down to the bottoms of his feet, I knew him so well, and I loved every part of him. His big blue eyes, his long eyelashes, his thick brown hair, his strong arms and shoulders, his tattoos; I loved his tattoos. My mind stopped at a single tattoo he had on his arm, Paul's powerful words from Philippians 1:21: "To live is Christ and to die is gain." Why did Andrew love that verse enough to get it permanently etched onto his arm? Why did it mean so much to him? What did it mean, anyway? This didn't feel like gain. It only felt like loss and pain. What did Paul mean when he penned these words thousands of years ago?

In his letter to Philippi, Paul said:

> I will rejoice, for I know that through your prayers and the help of the Spirit of Jesus Christ this will turn out for my deliverance, as it is my eager expectation and hope that I will not be at all ashamed, but that with full courage now as always Christ will be honored in my body, whether by life or by death. *For to me to live is Christ, and to die is gain.* If I am to live in the flesh, that means fruitful labor for me. Yet which I shall choose I cannot tell. I am hard pressed between the two. My desire is to depart and be with Christ, for that is far better. But to remain in the flesh is more necessary on your account. Convinced of this, I know that I will remain and continue with you all, for your progress and joy in the faith, so that in me you may have ample cause to glory in Christ Jesus, because of my coming to you again. (Phil. 1:18–26 ESV, emphasis mine)

It's the tug-of-war of life, isn't it? The push and pull between the here and now and the yet to come. The desire to live our one life fully is muddled with the desire to depart from this place of darkness and pain. When we lose someone we love, there are moments where the choice to stay and live is easy, but there are equally dark moments where we are left wondering, *What's the point, anyway?* Remaining in the flesh becomes, in Paul's words, "necessary."

"Hard pressed between the two"—that's how grief feels. That's how I felt at the cemetery picking out a plot for Andrew. One plot or two: an impossible decision with a long life ahead of me and countless questions racing through my mind. *Will I be one of the lucky ones who finds love again, or will Andrew always be my one and only? How do I make this decision now? Why him, why me, why my family? One plot or two?*

To live is Christ and to die is gain. The words echoed in my mind. To *live*. The choice to live was my only choice, and it's the bravest choice I've ever made. "One plot is all we need," I whispered under my breath. I then excused myself from the office. I knew Andrew wouldn't want me to give up now; I knew he hadn't wanted to die, but to live. I knew his death meant gain for him, even if it stripped everything from me. While he was rejoicing in eternity, I walked slowly through the tall trees of the cemetery to see the place where his body would be laid to rest. Tears rolled down my cheeks relentlessly. I was alive, but barely. I hadn't eaten in days, so my clothes draped loosely over my thin frame. I stood in the warm sun on the green grass near his little plot and thought about my choice to live.

To live for Christ, for him and his glory.

To live for my Andrew, to honor his name.

To live for my boys; they needed me now.

To live for my future; it needed me too.

To live because life is worth living.

To live is to suffer; it's part of being human. No one is exempt from the brokenness of this place; it touches all of us at some point. Although we would like it to be, life isn't fair. We can go through life making all the right decisions, but bad things will still happen to us. It's upside down, backward, and twisted. Bad things happen to seemingly good people all the time—cancer appears out of nowhere, babies are born without breath in their lungs, accidents happen in an instant. If I have learned anything from the loss of Andrew it's that our bodies are fragile. It's an absolute miracle that we live as long as we do. We are all just an inch, an accident, an illness, a misstep away from death. So how do we live? How do we live beyond the suffering?

"To live is Christ." To live fully dependent on Christ—that's the secret to living beyond the suffering. It's a secret Paul knew all too well because he had experienced hell on earth over and over again. Paul was able to discover joy in the pain, joy in the prison, joy in the impossible situation, only with Christ.

I always knew God, but I didn't know how much I needed him until I lost Andrew. In losing Andrew I gained a whole new dependence on Christ. I couldn't survive the loss or overcome the pain without him.

When I couldn't eat, he gave me sustenance.

When I couldn't see the next step, he paved the way.

When everything looked blurry and I couldn't make decisions, he gave me clarity.

When I couldn't stop crying, he held me in his arms.

When I didn't want to live, he gave me reasons to stay.

I lost Andrew, but I gained spiritual depth.

I lost Andrew, but I gained perspective.

I lost Andrew, but I gained wisdom.

I lost Andrew, but I gained a new life.

It was a new life I didn't want. No matter how many times I tried to go back, the only way forward was forward. I continued to process my grief out loud through blogs, and I buried myself in books and therapy. I will never forget a saying my counselor shared in one of our first sessions following Andrew's death: "We cannot direct the wind, but we can adjust our sails." What happened to Andrew, what happened to us, was out of my control. I didn't choose this, I didn't choose loss, but I did have the opportunity to choose how I would respond. The harsh reality, I learned early on, is loss requires adjusting.

After Andrew died, everything had to be reexamined. I realized the house we lived in wouldn't work anymore. It was too big, too much to manage on my own. So we packed up, moved out, and moved in with family. I was a stay-at-home mom, but I needed space to grieve and figure out what to do next. So I enrolled all three of the boys in school full-time. My identity as a pastor's wife was stripped away when Andrew was, so I faced the decision either to stay in a church I loved and find a new way to fit in or walk away and find a new church home. I'd become a single mom overnight. This was the biggest challenge—raising three boys, ages two, four, and five—all on my own. It was daunting. Life would never be the same for me or my boys. We were forced to grapple with a new reality that we had never planned for.

This is still our life. We are always adjusting. Things happen all the time that are beyond the realm of our understanding. As hard as we try to control our lives, the truth is only God has the ultimate power over life and death. I have discovered through my grief and pain that the only way to live is in surrender. *To live is Christ*, my life fully in his hands.

Surrender

Surrender, giving ourselves up into the power of another,[2] is a daily part of life. It is an act we do all the time without even realizing it. But the type of surrender God asks from us is different; it's sacred. He wants us to totally and completely give our lives to him, without holding anything back. Jesus said that when we finally let go and let God have control, we will actually recover our lives.

"Are you tired? . . . Come to me. Get away with me and you'll *recover your life*. I'll show you how to take a real rest. Walk with me and work with me—watch how I do it. Learn the unforced rhythms of grace. I won't lay anything heavy or ill-fitting on you. Keep company with me and you'll learn to live freely and lightly" (Matt. 11:28–30 THE MESSAGE, emphasis mine).

Isn't that amazing? Through surrender, through walking with God, we develop a new rhythm of grace. It's how we acquire the stamina necessary to live another day. Surrendering will require courage, strength, and grit, but it doesn't have to be complicated. It can be a simple act, such as whispering to God, "I can't, but you can."

When we surrender bad things will still happen, life will continue to throw hard, fast curveballs that bring us to our knees, but surrender means we don't have to find new footing on our own. He will hold us up when we do not have the strength to stand, and he will redeem our stories, either on this side of heaven or the other. There will be purpose even in our pain if we bravely choose him, choose joy, choose courage, choose life, and choose surrender.

When I think about surrender, I think about Psalm 139, my favorite psalm. I was introduced to it during my sophomore year of college when the local church I was attending started an event called "Third Wednesday." On the third Wednesday of each month, the church would hold three sessions a day for people to gather and seek God through fasting, worship, and prayer. At that time in my life, I was feeling far from God. The hype of freshman year had worn off, and as a sophomore, I felt lost and lonely. I decided to try to seek God in a new way and give this Third Wednesday experience a chance.

As I walked into the room, I felt insecure and skeptical, but I immediately knew I was supposed to be there. The chairs had been removed, the lights were low, and soft acoustic music filled the atmosphere. I found an empty space and sat down on the floor, soaking it all in. I felt the presence of God covering me like a thick warm blanket. Halfway through the session, a woman came to the stage and began to read a Bible passage I had never heard before. She asked us to close our eyes, relax our minds, and allow God's powerful Word to wash over us. I followed her lead and was instantly broken by the love of God. I felt a divine release.

This is Psalm 139:

You have searched me, LORD, and you know me. You know when I sit and when I rise; you perceive my thoughts from afar. You discern my going out and my lying down; you are familiar with all my ways. Before a word is on my tongue you, LORD, know it completely. You hem me in behind and before, and you lay your hand upon me. Such knowledge is too wonderful for me, too lofty for me to attain.

Where can I go from your Spirit? Where can I flee from your presence? If I go up to the heavens, you are there; if I make my bed in the depths, you are there. If I rise on the wings of the dawn, if I settle on the far side of the sea, even there your hand will guide me, your right hand will hold me fast. If I say, "Surely the darkness will hide me and the light become night around me," even the darkness will not be dark to you; the night will shine like the day, for darkness is as light to you.

For you created my inmost being; you knit me together in my mother's womb. I praise you because I am fearfully and wonderfully made; your works are wonderful, I know that full well. My frame was not hidden from you when I was made in the secret place, when I was woven together in the depths of the earth. Your eyes saw my unformed body; all the days ordained for me were written in your book before one of them came to be. How precious to me are your thoughts, God! How vast is the sum of them! Were I to count them, they would outnumber the grains of sand—when I awake, I am still with you.

... Search me, God, and know my heart; test me and know
my anxious thoughts. See if there is any offensive way in me, and
lead me in the way everlasting.

What God revealed to me through this psalm was the key to
unlocking a boundless relationship with him. I came to realize
he was always there; he never left me. Even when I felt alone, lost,
confused, angry, and sad, he was there. Even when life hadn't gone
the way I'd planned, he was there. Even when it felt like my friends
and my family had abandoned me, he was there. I discovered then
and I know now in the depths of my unrelenting pain that he is
there. The suffering of this world does not diminish his power. God
is near, and he makes his presence known through our suffering.

When we suffer, when we are in pain, when we are overcome
with grief, God suffers with us. He is not distant or detached. He is
near, and he shares in our suffering. There will never be sufficient
words to comfort, but the Word who became flesh is enough. Every
single worry, every single grief, every single pain, every single
doubt, every single bad, terrible thing—when we don't know what
to do, we can lay it all down at the feet of Jesus.

The Wilderness

We are able to suffer without being defeated because Jesus suf-
fered first. We can walk through the wilderness seasons because
he showed us the way. We can find our footing again and brush

off the dust because of his promise to work all things together for our good (Rom. 8:28).

After the angels attended to Jesus in the wilderness, he traveled to Galilee to begin his ministry, declaring, "The time has come" (Mark 1:15). He had passed the test of the wilderness, and God was ready to bring his ministry to earth through the literal hands and feet of Jesus. It was a plan millions of years in the making. God used the wilderness to prepare Jesus for his purpose.

What if our pain can serve a purpose too?

What if our wilderness is working a miracle deep inside our soul?

God knew when Jesus would be ready to start his ministry here on earth, and he also knew when it would be time to call Jesus home. As it was for Jesus, our time here is limited, but we serve a God who isn't limited by time. We can trust that in and through each season, each trial, each step in the wild of the wilderness, God is right there with us. And even the most devastating loss has the potential to be used as a part of his greater plan.

I don't have all of the answers, and I will never fully understand why God allowed Andrew to die at thirty years old the way he did, but I still have hope. I can pin my hope in God because I know if I lose hope, I lose everything. Life without hope is life without meaning. That first week after Andrew died is still a complete blur. The decisions I made were too many to count, the emotions too overwhelming to describe, and the gut-wrenching pain too deep to comprehend. But I still had hope. In my soul I knew God was still there, sitting right beside me, weeping with me, holding me through every moment of my pain. My mind was lost and confused, but in the center of the confusion, there was hope.

Hope beyond my circumstance.

Hope in my future.

Hope in heaven.

In the dark moments and days following Andrew's death, there was a delicate dance between hope and fear. The seed of hope was rooted deep within my soul but fear had run its course and destroyed my life. Fear had crept into our home and spread like wildfire. It had been fear gone wild, wild enough to take over everything.

The anxiety was rooted in fear.

The panic attacks were rooted in fear.

The depression was rooted in fear.

The spiritual warfare was rooted in fear.

And ultimately the suicide was rooted in fear.

Although we would like to live without it, we actually need fear. Fear protects us and stops us from making bad decisions. Fear tells us when something isn't right. Without fear, our lives would be filled with even more problems and pain. From the moment we are born we learn to fear certain things in this world in order to survive. Fear is part of being human.

We need fear to survive, but we also need hope—just enough fear to keep us grounded and just enough hope to keep us looking up. But how do we know which one is running the show? How do we know when fear has taken over and is running wild?

A FEW SIGNS FEAR MAY BE RULING OUR LIVES:
We settle for less.

Fear can cause us to shrink back from our dreams and aspirations. Fear is the tiny voice that whispers, "You could never do that. You aren't smart enough. You aren't talented enough. You aren't quali- fied enough. It will take too long. It won't happen for you." If we feel like we are settling for less, we can decide today to fight for more. We can stop allowing fear to control our dreams, and we can start to believe we are capable, we are smart, and we can do anything because with God, anything is possible.

We say yes when we want to say no.

Fear of letting people down can cause us to respond with a quick yes when it would be best to say no. We can't be everything to everyone all the time. When we try to be, we will become bitter, and resentment will build up in our hearts. The next time we feel the urge to say yes even though we want to say no, we can stop and ask ourselves, "What is motivating my response?" If the answer is fear, we can take control and decide to say no.

We seek to numb the pain.

Fear can cause deep inner pain, which can make us physically ill. Fear can manifest itself in anger, sadness, loneliness, and fatigue. We sometimes try to avoid the pain with temporary Band-Aids like alcohol, drugs, food, sex, work, television, or social media. Before we reach for empty relief, we can choose instead to pick up the phone and call a friend, get down on our knees and say a prayer, pull out a journal and write our thoughts, or turn off all of the noise and sit in solitude. When we create and seek healthy outlets for our pain, we minimize fear and create space for hope.

We want control.

Fear may cause us to feel the need to control everything and everyone around us. Especially when the fear is birthed from a place of trauma. We may believe that by having control we can actually prevent the bad, awful thing from happening again. To let go of control we must replace fear with faith. Faith that God keeps his promises and he will truly work everything together for our good.

We get sick.

Living under constant fear comes at a high cost. Fear can weaken the immune system, causing heart damage or intestinal problems such as irritable bowel syndrome and ulcers. Fear can decrease fertility, cause us to age at a faster rate, and even lead to premature death. Fear also has a powerful impact on the mind. Over a period of time fear can impair memory, cause brain damage, and even change the way our brains process information, which can cause us to make poor decisions, react irrationally, and respond negatively to the world around us. Long-term fear can lead to mental health complications such as clinical depression, fatigue, and PTSD.[3]

The word became flesh to conquer fear and death forever. Through the cross we have been given a living hope. We can choose to believe the same God who raised Jesus from the dead and shocked the entire world still has surprises in store for us. We can choose to believe, no matter how dark our circumstances, that we serve a God who always has one more move.

When the test results come in and it's not good, God still has one more move.

When the job falls through again and again, God still has one more move.

When it feels like everyone has abandoned us and we are all alone, God still has one more move.

When the pain is overwhelming and we want to give up completely, God still has one more move.

When suicide strikes and we feel like our lives are over too, God still has one more move.

The secret to conquering fear and death is safely securing our hope in him who always has one more move. To live as Christ, we will share in his suffering, but we will also share in his victory. Although we may lose everything we love in this world, with God we still win in the end. He is our living hope, drawing us home to heaven one breath, one moment, one day at a time.

NINE

New Wine

To my Andrew,

Tonight [is another night] at home without you. I see you all over this house, and there are a million little things that I see and remember that completely break my heart. I see you in the garage working out. I see you in the bed taking a nap. I see you in the kitchen drinking a protein shake. I see you at night sneaking Ben & Jerry's from the freezer. I see you in your office, quietly, confidently typing away, crafting another powerful message for Sunday.

The boys see you too. They see you outside doing yard work. They see you with your hammer and drill hanging things on the walls. They see you sitting on the couch watching a movie with them. They see you in the bed in the morning when they walk in to wake me up. They see you in the driveway picking weeds. They see you in our closet getting ready for work.

I don't know how to not see you here. You are a part of me. You are a part of our children. A special, important part. Life without you feels hopeless and heavy. I have countless unanswered questions, numerous broken dreams, and a myriad of shattered plans. The change feels painfully unnatural. I don't want the change; I just want you here with me. I want things to go back to the way they were before.

On the day I broke the news to the boys, Smith and I spent some time drawing together in a coloring book titled *When Someone I Love Dies*. It is a strange forced feeling to be discussing death with a 5, 4, and 2-year-old. I can see Smith's brain working tirelessly just like mine, attempting to wrap his young mind around this new reality.

Something unexpected that has been helping us this week is butterflies. You would probably laugh and make fun of us, but we can't seem to escape them. The first few pages of our new coloring book examined change. The book instructed us to draw an egg, a caterpillar, a cocoon, and then a butterfly. It was a simple way for a 5-year-old to understand that life is ever evolving, ever changing.

Just a few hours after we finished coloring, I went to close the curtains in the family room. To my surprise there was a tiny green caterpillar attached to the top part of the curtain. What is a caterpillar doing in our house? How did it crawl up so high on the curtain? The door has been closed all day; how did it end up there? Usually, I would have squealed and run away, but I was so stunned that I picked it up and showed the boys. Without skipping a beat Smith told me, "It's a miracle from God."

Smith, in his childlike faith, believed God sent us the precious little caterpillar to remind us that He is near. He is in the details. He is connected and He cares. I agreed with Smith, and we both cried over that little caterpillar. We quickly found a jar and some leaves and now we are taking great care of our new pet whom Smith named "Little Buddy." We now get to sit back and watch Little Buddy evolve and change before our eyes. . . .

In the midst of my quiet time this morning the image of a butterfly jumped out at me from a book. In the book [*Through the Eyes of a Lion*], the author [Levi Lusko] says, "I started to think a lot about butterflies and how if you cut them out of their cocoons or help them out in any way, they will never develop the strength they need in their wings to be able to achieve takeoff. They have to struggle out in order to come into their own. Flight only comes after the fight."[1]

Right now I feel like a caterpillar trapped in a dark cocoon. It feels like a full-on battle, a full-fledged war. I didn't choose this. I don't want this. I just want to be a caterpillar again. I don't want to be wrapped up in grief and pain, I don't want to walk through this. I don't want to be smothered by anxious thoughts about my future and the future of our children. I want this all to go away so I can be free again.

Today I am reminded that although I hate it, God has me right where I need to be. I can feel Him wrapping His loving arms around me. I am fighting it, kicking and screaming, but I can feel the Holy Spirit infusing me with His strength. I can feel God protecting me and holding me close. I can feel the safety and security in my own little cocoon. It may take years until I am ready to fly, but I know that the fight won't last forever. One day, God will release me from the darkness and despair. He will show me a life of hope and a future full of purpose. I will no longer be a carefree caterpillar. I will emerge a new creation, a beautiful butterfly, and I will soar to even greater heights. I can't see any of it now in my dark, clouded cocoon, but I know that I am safe. He's got me right where I need to be, and He has great plans for my life and the life of our boys.

"'For I know the plans I have for you,' declares the LORD, 'plans to prosper you and not to harm you, plans to give you hope and a future'" (Jer. 29:11).

> I miss you, Andrew, I miss you so much. I love you,
>
> Your Girl[2]

Caterpillars and butterflies. I never knew how much I could relate to something that I counted insignificant before Andrew's death. Sure, I had noticed a butterfly fluttering through the air and for a moment thought it beautiful, but there was never a caterpillar that stopped me in my tracks—not until the day a "miracle from God" came so clearly in the form of a tiny green caterpillar.

It meant everything.

It was a miracle.

It was a promise from God.

A reminder he is real, he hears our cries, he sees our pain, he cares about every intricate detail of our lives, and he isn't far but near. A reminder that miracles come in all shapes and sizes and life itself is one beautiful miracle. Breathing in and out, the sights, the sounds, the smells, the tastes of this one life—it's all a gift.

When we lose someone we love, it changes the way we see the world. When Andrew died, I began to notice things I hadn't noticed before. I began to look for little glimpses, little miracles, little kisses from heaven everywhere. The clouds in the sky, the sunset in the evening, and the waves crashing at the beach all stirred new awe and wonder in my soul. A childlike faith awakened deep inside, and for months I spent my days searching everywhere for signs of heaven, of Andrew, of something more, of something beyond this place. While driving, I would pull over to the side of the road just to stare at the sky. I would play with my kids in the backyard and completely lose myself in the beauty of the dwindling daylight. I would sit on my paddleboard in the ocean and imagine Andrew sitting on the perfect shores of eternity.

Andrew and I were one. We had a deep soul connection. When he left this place, he took half of my heart with him, and it changed me. My old life died. What once was one had torn in two, and in the tearing, God was preparing a new heart for me. This was an intricate open-heart surgery, and the recovery would take years. I often wondered if my heart would ever find its rhythm again.

The fear that had crept into Andrew's mind and torn our world apart led me to a new wilderness. A new life, a new terrain to navigate, far away from what I knew to be home. Andrew was my home. Now I felt like a wanderer, forced to build a new home in a foreign land. A new heart, a new home, a new life. And this new life was graced with a new calling. I knew it, I felt it, God made it very clear—my pain would not be wasted. There would be a wellspring in the wilderness, new life in a desolate place.

A wellspring is a beginning, a source, a root, a fountainhead through which life overflows. The immediate, overwhelming, punch-in-the-gut pain of loss couldn't be a wellspring, could it? A wellspring is a source of life, and death signifies the end of life; they couldn't be more opposite. Like joy and sorrow, you couldn't have both at the same time—could you?

If I have learned anything from the trenches of loss, it's that nothing makes sense. Everything is upside down and backward, and emotions are scattered all over the place. How you expect to feel isn't how you actually feel, and how you actually feel isn't how you want to feel at all. I have also learned joy and sorrow can co-exist, and there are springs and streams to be found on the desolate plains of pain.

It's a pressing, crushing, transforming process, being thrust into a new life, a new calling, a new world. It has the potential to destroy us completely or change us deeply. Like the caterpillar, we may have never asked to become a butterfly. Maybe we were happy with our life the way it was. We didn't ask to soar to greater heights or to live a life of greater calling or to be given deeper beauty.

Even though life wasn't always easy, I was happy with the way things were. I was happy with where Andrew and I were headed. I loved my life. If you had asked me where I saw myself in twenty years, I would have confidently answered like this: "Living in the same beautiful house, serving at the same beautiful church, married to the same beautiful man, and raising the same beautiful boys." That's all I wanted. I had all I could ever ask for and more. I wasn't looking for a new life.

But life is always changing, always evolving, always shifting, always moving, and if I have learned anything through this process, it's that control is just an illusion, a façade. Life isn't predictable; it's unpredictable. The plans we make aren't set in stone; instead they are like putty in God's hands. He takes the caterpillar and transforms it into a beautiful butterfly. It isn't the caterpillar's decision, but *his*. In the lifecycle of a caterpillar, this is called the transition stage. This stage can last a few weeks up to a few years depending on the species. All of the work in the transition phase takes place inside the chrysalis.[3] On the outside it may appear as though nothing is happening; the naked eye is blind to the process taking place inside. It's intimate work, intricate work, important work: a Creator and his creation working it out together.

Just as the transition stage is necessary for the caterpillar to become a butterfly, it is also a necessary step in grief. Loss beckons each of us to curl up for a while and rest in our own little chrysalis. Just as our grief is unique, our chrysalis is too. Maybe your chrysalis is sitting on the couch with a soft blanket and a Bible. Or maybe it's sitting down for coffee with a friend. Or maybe it's sitting with a box of tissues in the counselor's office. Or snuggling up in your bed and resting your body. For me it's been all of the above; the grief has followed me everywhere. I have been wrapped up in the pain no matter where I go.

The Journey of Grief

One place I have found rest and intimate connection with God is at the beach. Everything about the beach is healing to my soul. Almost weekly I find myself out on the water on a paddleboard. In a season where I don't know who I am anymore, where I feel numb and empty, something about being out on the water reminds me I'm alive. The wind in my face, the cold salty sea splashing all around, my muscles being pushed to the limit as I paddle—these things are life-giving to me. The experience is grounding, and it reminds me to feel again: to feel connected here on earth, to feel the presence of God, and to feel the pull of heaven.

As I sit on the water, I often find myself wondering about heaven.

Can Andrew experience what I am experiencing?

Is there an ocean in heaven?

Is there paddleboarding in heaven?

What is he doing right now?

What does it feel like?

Although I can only imagine what Andrew is experiencing in heaven, I do have the gift of what he left behind. Because Andrew was a pastor, he left us with a powerful, incredible, beautiful gift: his messages. Anytime I am overwhelmed with missing him, I can see him, hear him, and learn from him. These messages are healing right here and now, but they will also be an irreplaceable source of comfort for my boys as they grow and mature. When their memories start to fade and they have questions about their daddy, I can open up a message and press play. His humor, his mannerisms, his gifts, and his calling can all be on display with the click of a button. What a blessing.

There is one message in particular I replay often. It's a message Andrew gave on grief during a church-wide study on endurance.[4] Through the Endurance message series, Andrew taught our church how to withstand various trials in life. During his third sermon on the topic, Andrew addressed how to endure grief well. Every time I play this message, tears stream down my face. I remember sitting in the front row and watching Andrew give this message live, and now through his message he is teaching me how to grieve his death.

As I listen to his message, I am reminded that grief is part of life. It will hit all of us at some point. Some of us are on the front end of grief, and we are sitting in shock. Some of us are in the middle of grief, and we still feel numb. Some of us are on the back side of grief, and we've discovered that just because we move forward doesn't mean we move on; the grief will always be there. No matter where we find ourselves on the grief journey, here are a few truths about grief.

GRIEF IS UNAVOIDABLE

The consequence of love is grief. Every time we choose to love, we choose to grieve. True love means giving a part of ourselves away, and it is not easily retrieved. If we love someone or something we will grieve. If we ascribe value to someone or something we will grieve. If we've given our heart to someone or something we will grieve. Jesus said, "Very truly I tell you, you will weep and mourn while the world rejoices. You will grieve" (John 16:20).

GRIEF IS PAINFUL

It is difficult, impossible even, to accurately describe the pain of grief, but we try. C. S. Lewis described grief's all-encompassing power as "like the sky, spread over everything."[5] It is painful and lonely, isolating and torturous. Grief changes us, transforms us, and gives us new eyes to see everything. We learn to navigate our new normal through living with the pain. It's a pain we may carry for the rest of our lives. At first the pain may feel huge and overwhelming, but over time, as we heal, it can grow smaller.

I recently came across an analogy for grief, and it resonated deeply with me. It describes grief as a ball in a box. Also inside the box is a button. The box is our life, the ball is our grief, and the button is our pain. When the grief hits initially, it's so big and so overwhelming that every time we move the box rattles, and the ball taps the button relentlessly. However, over time the ball of grief begins to shrink on its own. As we live and move and breathe the grief still rattles around inside, but because it has gotten smaller, it hits the pain button less often. As time passes and we seek healing for our grief, the ball continues to shrink. It rarely hits the pain button. We may be able to make it through a day or even an entire week without feeling the intensity of the pain. But when it does hit, the pain is just as strong as it was the first time we felt it. It's just as hard to understand.[6] We may never be fully released from the pain this side of heaven, but maybe, as we learn to live with the grief, it will grow a little smaller—one day at a time.

The Ball and the Box

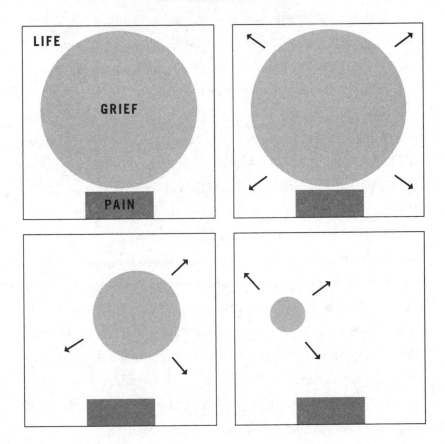

GRIEF IS TEMPORAL

"Now is your time of grief, but I will see you again and you will rejoice, and no one will take away your joy" (John 16:22). When the pain is overwhelming, we can choose to lose heart, or we can choose to remember our joy is truly anchored. My joy is not anchored in Andrew, my joy is not anchored in my children, and my joy is not anchored in my future. The only safe, sacred place where I can find unconditional love and securely anchor my joy is with God. No matter what kind of grief we are facing, we don't have to face it alone. We can choose to invite God's supernatural peace, joy, and love into our pain. When we do, maybe we will discover that, although the pain we feel now is temporal, joy is eternal.

I love these encouraging words from Jesus: "I have told you these things, so that in me you may have peace. In this world you will have trouble. But take heart! I have overcome the world" (v. 33). We will grieve, but we will also live, and to live is the miracle. Whether we have eyes to see them or not, miracles surround us. As God gave me new vision through pain, I began to notice evidence of his miracle work everywhere. I was so blown away by the presence and provision of God that I started making a list of the miracles I saw so I would never forget all the incredible work he's done. These are small and large reminders that the God we serve is intimate and intentional. I knew God was real before Andrew died, but the way he showed up so clearly after Andrew's death only bolstered my faith. I cried over the loss of my husband, but I also shed tears over the pure goodness of God.

The Wilderness

After Jesus' time in the wilderness, he went on to perform his first miracle. I find this truly fascinating. It parallels so intimately with my story. When we were in our wilderness season with Andrew's mental illness, we were begging God for a miracle. I will never forget sitting at our favorite lifeguard tower, Tower 52 in Newport Beach, huddled up in the sand together, begging God to lift the darkness and heal Andrew completely. But God didn't show up the way we wanted him to. The truth is, he actually allowed the dark, confusing wilderness season to continue. And ultimately, he allowed Andrew to die. But as soon as Andrew left our lives, God was everywhere, in everything, all of the time. I was surrounded by his mighty presence, and it was beautiful and sacred yet also frustrating and confusing.

We have all had our fair share of wilderness seasons, haven't we? Seasons where we are begging God to show up, but it feels like he is ignoring us completely. Why does God sometimes go silent? Why does he sometimes wait until after the wilderness to allow the miracles? I don't know the answer, and I don't know if I will ever know why this side of heaven. The unanswerable *why* question is the mystery of God, the mystery of faith. I wrestle with the *why* all the time. *Why* Andrew? *Why* me? *Why* our family? *Why* now?

When I have exhausted myself with the why, I sit in surrender, releasing the why back to him and acknowledging, "There's nothing I can do." I'm sure most of us wish the hard, terrible thing would just go away and God wouldn't ask so much of us. If we could write the script of our lives, we would skip past the ugly and uncomfortable and fast-forward to the good, the happy, the easy. But there is something sacred about showing up to fight for our story. It's in the fight that God stitches our one broken heart back together with new strength, new power, new peace. In every unseen moment he is carefully guiding the needle and the thread.

And with each slow stitch we discover a hidden truth: healing is hard and holy, beautiful and painful, all at the same time.

As I sit in the slow, grueling process of grief, I am learning to breathe again. It's an everyday exhale, an everyday letting go, an everyday crying out, an everyday release of what was. I have no choice after I exhale but to inhale. To inhale: new hope, new peace, new truth, new joy—new life.

I am learning that God doesn't work in my timeline, so I must surrender to his. When we are in a season of waiting, instead of trying to fast-forward the process, maybe we can pray this simple prayer of surrender: "God, make me what I should be in the midst of my affliction, and help me to learn how to live here for as long as it may last."[7] Every day in the wilderness, our souls are developing the patient endurance that can only come from deep discomfort. By drawing near to the presence of God, we are able to show up to our present reality.

I love how Paul described the patient endurance of waiting on God. He wrote, "But that's not all! Even in times of trouble we have a joyful confidence, knowing that our pressures will develop in us patient endurance. And patient endurance will refine our character, and proven character leads us back to hope. And this hope is not a disappointing fantasy, because we can now experience the endless love of God cascading into our hearts through the Holy Spirit who lives in us!" (Rom. 5:3–5 TPT).

The pain and pressures of life develop endurance. Endurance refines us as it slowly shapes and transforms us into something new. After Jesus endured the wilderness, he went on to create something new too—out of nothing he created something. His first miracle: new wine. I love this story because it is such a beautiful picture of what God can do in and through our pain. God wants to make new wine in all of us. He wants to bring us from the wilderness to the promise.

Three days later there was a wedding in the village of Cana in Galilee. Jesus' mother was there. Jesus and his disciples were guests also. When they started running low on wine at the wedding banquet, Jesus' mother told him, "They're just about out of wine."

Jesus said, "Is that any of our business, Mother—yours or mine? This isn't my time. Don't push me."

She went ahead anyway, telling the servants, "Whatever he tells you, do it."

Six stoneware water pots were there, used by the Jews for ritual washings. Each held twenty to thirty gallons. Jesus ordered the servants, "Fill the pots with water." And they filled them to the brim.

"Now fill your pitchers and take them to the host," Jesus said, and they did.

When the host tasted the water that had become wine (he didn't know what had just happened but the servants, of course, knew), he called out to the bridegroom, "Everybody I know begins with their finest wines and after the guests have had their fill brings in the cheap stuff. But you've saved the best till now!"

This act in Cana of Galilee was the first sign Jesus gave,

the first glimpse of his glory. And his disciples believed in him.
(John 2:1–11 THE MESSAGE)

This story is about a sign: the old is gone, and the new has come. The wine was a symbol, a sacred act, a sacred moment. It indicated the kingdom of God had arrived. It was the beginning of new miracles, new signs and wonders, and a new redemption story being written through the life and ministry of Jesus, the one who came to save us all forever. Jesus didn't just make any wine; he made the best wine, and he made it in abundance.

How symbolic is this for our own lives, for our own wilderness seasons? God doesn't just want to make new wine in us; he wants to make *the best wine*. When we open the door to our heart and invite him into our most vulnerable, sacred space, he is able to give us new, abundant life. I love these words from Paul's prayer at the end of his letter to the Ephesians: "Now to him who is able to do far more abundantly than all that we ask or think, according to the power at work within us" (Eph. 3:20 ESV). When we plant our feet firmly in God's gentle, unfailing love, we can experience abundant life—even in our deepest pain.

I have found this to be true in my grief journey as I have encountered God's abundant love over and over again. One of these abundant love encounters happened to be an invitation for the boys and me to travel to Israel. The trip itself was a gift, but God also orchestrated every detail. The trip fell on my thirtieth birthday and on Father's Day, our first Father's Day without Andrew. I don't think it's a coincidence we just so happened to be in Israel that week. And I don't think it was by chance that on Father's Day we had the opportunity to be baptized in the Jordan River, the same place where Jesus declared his love for his Father. The last place Jesus stood before his wilderness journey. It wasn't a coincidence; it was a beautiful gift. God knew Father's Day would hurt, and he wanted it to be different. Not because we're special or because we deserve it at all, but because the love he offers is abundant, above and beyond anything we could ever dream up on our own.

So, on Father's Day we threw on some baggy white robes and walked hand in hand into the water to receive the gift of redemption. It was my absolute honor to baptize my sons, Smith and Jethro, to the Father on Father's Day. The Father who loves them more than Andrew ever could. The Father who knew them before they were born and will be with them wherever they go. The Father they can always count on no matter what life throws their way. I am so grateful for the gift we received that day, a powerful new Father's Day memory.

We will walk through pain in this life, but we will never walk alone. We serve a God who wants to be invited in and desires nothing more than to write a new redemption story in and through our pain. "To the fatherless he is a father. To the widow he is a champion friend. To the lonely he makes them part of a family. To the prisoners he leads into prosperity until they sing for joy. This is our Holy God in his Holy Place!" (Ps. 68:5 TPT).

TEN

Rebuilding Beautiful

To my Andrew,

Six months. Unbelievable. It can't be real. I still can't understand how you are gone. I look through old pictures and you come alive. I can hear your voice. I can see your mannerisms. I can run my fingers through your scruffy beard and lay my head to rest on your strong shoulder. I can clearly picture us sitting in your truck, holding hands, driving off together on our date night, not saying much but simply being present in the moment, just us.

If I close my eyes tight enough, you're here sitting right beside me: strong, resilient you. My defender, my provider, my protector, my beautiful other half, I miss you.

Time is really strange. It's almost as if it has sped up since you've been gone. So much time has passed and so much life has happened, yet it feels like you were just here. You were just riding skateboards in the driveway with the boys and planting new flowers in the backyard. You were just sitting in your office working, dreaming, praying, and planning out our future. You were just lying beside me at night, keeping me safe and warm.

And then you left. So abruptly, you left. I will never understand why. Every time I try to make sense of it all, I crumble to the floor. You didn't want to die, you wanted to live. You loved me and the boys so much. You didn't want to cause us pain. I know you were hurting. Andrew, I am so sorry I didn't fully understand. I am so sorry I wasn't right beside you that morning, rubbing your back and reminding you of who you are. Every day I wish I wasn't waking up to this reality. Every day I miss you more. . . .

The boys miss you so much, Andrew. We talk about you every night before they go to bed. I call it our "daddy talk." They share special memories of you. Their favorite thing to share is that one time you pooped your pants when you were sick. They laugh really hard. Every memory is a gift you gave them. I am so grateful they remember you for who you are, their amazing daddy. Smith reminds me so much of you. He is a deep thinker; he is creative, and you would love this: he's obsessed with basketball! It's all he wants to do! Your sweet buddy Jethro, the one who had your heart, you had such a special connection with him, he is growing up. He has a new girlfriend every week, he learned how to write his name, he is starting to ride his bike without training wheels, and he still looks the most like you. And Brave, our sweet boy, he is still our baby. He is sensitive, kind, and gentle. He is talking a lot more now and is still really passionate about monster trucks; his favorite is the "mohawk monster truck." You can't help but smile when you look at him; he's a precious gift.

And I'm still here. Somehow by the grace of God managing to get out of bed every morning and walk this out one day at a time. It's really painful. My whole life died with you. I was handed a blank canvas the day you died. Not knowing how it would ever become beautiful again. Yet, here I stand, six months later, staring at the blank canvas, starting to see tiny bits of color. God, the master artist, the one who holds the brush, is stroke by stroke creating something new: a brand-new life, a brand-new work of art. While the blank space still stretches far across the canvas, a new picture is beginning to emerge. It will take time to become beautiful again; it will take a lifetime, but a lifetime isn't forever. Forever is with you, and I can't wait to meet you there.

Until then, I promise to make you proud, raise our boys to be godly men, and continue to spread the message "God's got this." Because He does.

Love,
Your Girl[1]

As much as Andrew loved to work with his mind, he equally loved to work with his hands. It was his way of resting, his sabbath, his refueling. When he had a day to himself he would fill it with house projects. Over the course of our nearly eight-year marriage, we lived in four different homes. Each home was special, each home holds unique memories and milestones, but there is one home in particular that will always have a special place in my heart. It's the first home we ever purchased on our own: a small one-story in Chino, California, on the corner of a quiet, well-established neighborhood. The kind of neighborhood with neighbors who wave when you drive by, drop cookies off on the front porch just because, and throw big parties in the streets for the Fourth of July.

The house wasn't perfect. It was actually far from perfect. It had an obnoxious blue garage door, two bright blue front doors to match, stained carpet, popcorn ceilings, a green pool, an outdated kitchen, and wires coming out of the walls in every room. But as soon as we walked through those bright blue front doors, we knew we had found our home. We put in an offer before the house even hit the market, and just a few months later we received the keys. Primed with countless trips to the local Home Depot, hours on Pinterest, and a hundred DIY YouTube videos, we decided to roll up our sleeves and remodel it ourselves before we moved in. Andrew, with the help of family and friends, ripped out the carpet, painted the walls, pulled out the wires, patched the holes, and replaced the flooring—all within a week. The day we moved in, it felt like we were moving into a brand-new home. Andrew, with his strong will, brilliant mind, and skillful hands, had rebuilt beautiful from the ground up.

Those early memories, those special days when it was just Andrew, Smith, and me moving into our first home, feel like a different lifetime, a different life. The memories, the moments, the snapshots of days with Andrew are all captured in the years *before*. Before life lost its color, before all of the dreams shattered, before my heart was ripped in two. I would do anything to go back to *before*, but I can't. I live in the tension of before and after, forced beyond my will to say goodbye to *before* and pushed toward accepting *after*. The hard, lonely, exhausting, depressing reality of *after*. I don't want to accept it. I want to reject it; I want to trade it in for a different life. Every day I wake up alone, raise three grieving boys alone, fix up a new house alone, and figure out how to live this new life alone. Alone is lonely, alone is painful, and alone feels far from beautiful.

Beauty after loss is like a game of hide-and-seek. Each new day I wake up searching for beautiful, believing if I look hard enough, I will find it. Believing if I find enough of it, somehow, it will cover up all of the ugly empty. I don't have to look far to find beauty; beauty lives in my home, in my boys: in their big blue eyes, their warm, gentle hugs, their innocent giggles, their precious little hands, their chubby cheeks, their peaceful sleep. They are the purest form of beauty, and God gave me three. Maybe he knew I would need three beautiful reasons to pull back the covers and step into this new life every day. My boys will never be able to take away my pain, but they give me a million reasons to stay.

Walking with my children through tragedy is the most painful thing I have ever done. Loss is woven into who we are as a family. Andrew's death is a part of our daily life and conversations. At school, it isn't uncommon for my boys to receive questions from their peers about why and how their daddy died. Questions a three-, five-, and seven-year-old should never be asked to answer. No matter how hard I try, I will never be able to shield them from the questions and the pain. The reality is, loss is a lifelong process, and we are each on our own unique healing journey.

I will never forget the first time I took my son Smith to the cemetery. The surreal reality of watching him process the gravity of death as his small fingers slowly traced every single letter on Dave's, his Papa's, headstone. Letters that spelled our last name. His family. His papa and his daddy. Two people he deeply loved, two of his best friends, just a few plots apart, both gone way too soon.

As I stood watching my son, images flashed through my mind of life *before*. Of Smith and Papa playing in the backyard together, Papa towing a little red wagon behind his wheelchair with Smith sitting proudly inside. Both wearing matching bucket hats, Smith covered from head to toe in dirt, and Papa with a genuine smile stretched across his face. Of Smith and his daddy mowing the lawn together. Andrew in a tank top and swim shorts, pushing his bright-green lawn mower. Smith with a backward baseball cap on his head, a Home Depot apron filled with tools strapped around his waist, and a small, bright-green lawn mower of his own following close behind. A patient daddy and his little boy doing chores and making memories together. The snapshots of life before loss, before two people who made our world beautiful left us behind. Two men who were pillars of our family. So much loss in just a few years, so much for Smith's precious young mind to comprehend.

I wrote a letter to Smith the day I took him there. We sat on a small bench next to Andrew's plot and I read him these words:

To my brave little warrior,
This is hard. Your first time here at this place. This is all so much to absorb, the earth-shattering, life-altering, heavy, ugly

brokenness. The daddy who played basketball with you in the backyard, taught you how to ride a bike, took you on dates to the movies, comforted you when you were sad, and made you laugh until you cried. His body, his empty shell, just a few feet below your feet. Your beautiful mind slowly grasping the raw reality. Real, tangible brokenness. I'm so sorry.

I just want you to know I am so proud of you, your daddy is so proud of you, and you are incredibly brave. Thank you for asking tough questions, thank you for helping me manage your brothers, thank you for hugging me when I'm sad and for loving me at my lowest. I just want you to know you don't have to be so strong. I know you're sad and broken. I'm sad and broken too. God's got big plans for you, son. You are creative, athletic, inquisitive, and brilliant, just like your dad. I can't wait to see how God uniquely uses you to change the world. I love you, Smitty.

Love,

Mom

Tears streamed down both of our cheeks as we hugged tight on our little bench. I explained to Smith that when Andrew died, he received a new body, an even better body, a body that will never break, a body that will never get sick, a body that will never have a headache or pass a kidney stone, a perfect body for a perfect place. We both smiled at the thought of our favorite guy flexing his new strong muscles in his new perfect body, building a new perfect home for us all to be together again one day. And for a moment we saw beauty in the *after*, beauty beyond the grave.

Every time I visit Andrew's quiet resting place, I sit on the same bench and think about time. The small weathered bench is our spot now, the closest place on earth to him. I don't visit very often, only when the pull is strong and I have no choice but to go. Sometimes I sit quietly without saying a word, other times it feels like the words will never stop. Benches, I've discovered, are an important part of the process. They beckon us to stop and rest for a while. They change our perspective and provide a safe space to take a deep breath and find our bearings again. They remind us all that life is a marathon, not a sprint.

From my bench I can see hundreds of headstones. Each stone engraved with time, each life marked between two dates, a beginning and an end. So many thoughts race through my mind. *What do we do with the dash in the middle? Why do I get more time?*

The first year after Andrew's death I was determined to fill my dash with beautiful. I made a promise to myself and my boys that we would have a "happy, beautiful life," and I was willing to chase after it as fast and as hard as I could. I accepted nearly every invitation to places all over the world. I traveled more in one year than I had in my whole life. I climbed the Sydney Harbour Bridge in the pouring rain. I sat with my boys on a large wooden boat in the Sea of Galilee. We ate cupcakes at Magnolia Market in Texas. We watched dancers throw fire at a luau in Kauai. I wrote words for this book at the top of a high-rise in Miami. We took a train ride with Santa through the Rocky Mountains of Colorado. Every opportunity a chance to reclaim beautiful, a chance to reclaim what was lost, a chance to fulfill the promise I made to us all. A chase, a hunt, a journey to discover new beautiful, new happy, new life.

Out of all of the trips we took the first year, there is one I will always hold close to my heart—the first one. It was the first brave yes, the first time I traveled across the country alone, my first trip without Andrew. My new friend Bob Goff had graciously invited me to Dream Big, a workshop he was hosting at a place called Onsite in Tennessee. A workshop where people from all over the world would come together to grow, learn, and dream again.

I was only a few months post loss, and I was living a life of shattered dreams. How could I possibly be ready to dream again? How could I even think about dreaming big? I didn't know the answer, but I knew I had to say yes. Saying yes meant choosing to believe there would be life after loss, hope after loss, dreams after loss, and beauty after loss.

I boarded an airplane, flew far away from home, followed a GPS through Nashville out to the countryside, and found myself at the beautiful Onsite campus. A place where people travel from all over the world to find healing and hope. A refuge for broken people like me to find fresh strength to carry on. Dream Big is just one of the many workshops they host on the Onsite campus. I wiped away my tears, pulled my suitcase out of the trunk, and stepped into my future, into new life, and into dreaming again.

Over the next few days I wanted to soak in every moment. I made new friends, shared my story for the first time, and discovered new dreams hidden deep inside my heart. During one of the workshop sessions, we stopped to write a letter to ourselves. A letter the team would later send in the mail to remind us all of our hopes and dreams.

This is what I wrote:

Dear Kayla,

Dream big. You can do anything you set your mind to. You are beautiful, you are loved, you are seen, you are heard, you have a heavenly Father who loves you more than any man ever will. You are going to go through hard things in life, but don't let those things knock you down. Get back up! Shake off the dust! Take a deep breath and move. Your life matters, your story matters, you are surrounded by people who love you deeply. Be a good friend, be a good mom, have fun with your kids! Take your kids on adventures. Your kids love you so much. They need you. Be present with them, have fun with them, take them to see the world. Speak truth into their life and love them to death. Love God, love others. Put others first. Find ways to help people who are hurting. Those people need to hear what you have to say. Your voice matters. You have something to say. You are wonderfully and beautifully made. God has a divine purpose for your life. You may not see it right now, but you are going to make a difference. People are going to come to know Jesus because of you. Lives will be changed, lives will be saved, the landscape of eternity will look different because of the way God is going to use you. Be fearless! Don't ever let fear hold you back. You do not need to be afraid of anything. Be loud, be you, be bold, be unique, be different, see who God sees and be her!

You are honored, you are chosen, and you are loved. You've got this because God's got this!

Love,

Kayla

Wouldn't it be beautiful if we could speak to ourselves this way all the time? If only we could see the beauty we already possess, the intrinsic beauty God so intimately designed and delicately placed in our unique DNA. We can stop searching tirelessly for beauty when we discover it already dwells within us. We are all beautiful vessels writing unrepeatable stories, stories that matter right now, stories worth fighting for.

Through my time at Dream Big, I learned that dreaming is at the heart of rebuilding. To rebuild we must dare to dream beyond the destruction. When I think about the word *rebuild*, I think about my precious, weary days as a stay-at-home mom, sitting on the rug, passing the time, playing blocks with my boys. Each time we would create a tall tower, someone would knock the whole thing down. Sometimes there would be hurt feelings, and other times we would all just burst out laughing. But every time we would build again. We would search around the floor, pick up all of the scattered pieces, and build something new. Each new creation would take a different shape, reach a different height, and develop a unique style of its own.

Now, here in our pain, we are rebuilding once again. We are gathering up all of the shattered pieces from every corner of our broken hearts and building something new together. Just like our toy towers, this new life will take on a new shape, reach a new height, and develop a new style of its own. It will never look the same as it did before, but we are choosing to believe beauty is still possible.

Breaking and rebuilding, falling down and getting back up again. It's who we are; it's who we have always been. None of us have arrived. None of us have it all figured out. It's what makes us human—and it's okay to be human. To be human is to experience it all: the ups and downs, the ebbs and flows, the highs and lows, the scattered in-between. It's all part of life—wild, broken, beautiful life—and it's all okay. To feel is to be alive, and to be alive is a gift. A gift we take for granted until we lose a life we love. Loss reminds us of our expiration date, a reminder we need from time to time. Our feelings now will end one day, and our end will be the beginning of new life somewhere else, somewhere far better than this. For this short time now, we can take a deep breath and whisper to ourselves, "It's okay." It's okay to feel all of the feelings we need to feel right now, and it's okay if the rebuilding doesn't happen overnight. We must give ourselves permission to be human.

When we whisper "It's okay," we replace shame with grace, and grace is the best gift we could ever give ourselves. Grace to be real with how we feel, all of the time. We all need more grace, more empathy, more space to feel. Without grace we will spend our one life always wishing things were different, and we will forget it's all a gift. Every single memory, every single day, every single moment, every single breath—a beautiful, precious gift. The gift of being alive.

Rebuilding, beginning again, is a daring choice. Just because we choose to begin again doesn't signify an end. Because there is no end, there is no goodbye—there is no moving on or letting go. There is only moving forward with the pain. Loss requires tension. We have to mourn, but we also have to keep on living the life God has given us. The pain of Andrew's death will stay with me for the rest of my life, but I can choose to build a beautiful landscape around it.

The Wilderness

There is a question we can each stop and ask ourselves when we walk through unavoidable trials in this life. It's a powerful question I believe fits the rebuilding while clearly acknowledging the suffering. It's a question Jesus asked his closest friends, his disciples, just hours before he would pay the ultimate price for us all. He said these words to Peter: "Shall I not drink the cup the Father has given me?" (John 18:11). What I love about Jesus and what makes him human is before he asked this question, before he ultimately submitted to the will of the Father, he wrestled.

He wrestled with his reality.

He wrestled with his purpose.

He wrestled with his mission.

He wrestled with the pain he knew was right around the corner.

He was fully God, but he was also fully human. And just like it isn't easy for us to accept our circumstances, it also wasn't easy for him. In his wrestling, Jesus begged God to take the cup away. "'Abba, Father,' he said, 'everything is possible for you. Take this cup from me. Yet not what I will, but what you will'" (Mark 14:36). Jesus was literally on his knees with his face to the ground, pleading with God to change his circumstances, to save him from the pain he knew was coming. He was pressed to the absolute limit physically, emotionally, and spiritually, to the point of sweating blood. Yet he was still willing to reach out his hand and accept the cup.

This picture of Jesus' suffering can bring us comfort in our pain. It's a reminder that even for Jesus, the son of God, remaining faithful to the end was deeply painful. And just as he wrestled with God, it's okay for us to wrestle too.

We may wrestle with accepting our "cup."

We may wrestle with pain.

We may wrestle with illness.

We may wrestle with loss and grief.

We may wrestle all throughout our lives with circumstances that are beyond our control, because we don't always get to choose our trials. We don't always get to decide how life pans out. Sometimes God will hand us a cup that is completely overwhelming, but he promises we will not have to carry it on our own. "Don't panic. I'm with you. There's no need to fear for I'm your God. I'll give you strength. I'll help you. I'll hold you steady, keep a firm grip on you" (Isa. 41:10 THE MESSAGE).

I have no idea what your cup looks like or how jagged its edges may be. I have no idea what it's like to live with the pain you are living with. But I do know that we do not have to carry our pain alone and that peace is possible. God wants to invade every area of our pain and brokenness with his perfect peace, but we have to posture our hearts to receive him. Maybe posturing our hearts looks like listening to worship music in the car in the morning. Or maybe posturing our hearts looks like going for a walk outside. Or maybe posturing our hearts is sitting with a cup of coffee and reading the Bible at the kitchen counter in the early hours of the morning before anyone else is awake. Or maybe posturing our hearts looks like Jesus in the garden. Maybe the pain is so overwhelming that it beckons us to our knees, it beckons us to the foot of the cross. And maybe today is the day when we declare that although we are broken, we aren't going to stay broken. We are going to choose to rebuild again, we are going to choose to accept the cup, and we are going to choose to bravely step into another day because we are still alive and God isn't finished with us yet.

As I have learned to accept my cup instead of walking away, I have received supernatural peace even in my pain. I have peace because I have seen God show up, I have seen his mighty hand at work, I have witnessed his miracles, and I have reaped the benefits of his favor and his blessing in and through my heartbreak. I still have pain, but I am confident God is using my pain for his purpose, he is using my story for his glory, and he has great plans for my life beyond the death of Andrew.

My life will always be defined by *before* and *after*, before Andrew died and after Andrew died, but it can still be beautiful. Even though after will never be the same as it was before, I can still choose to gather up the shattered pieces and build again. I can choose to own the story God is writing right now, and I can choose to believe my story, his story, will one day be beautiful.

ELEVEN

God's Got This

To my Andrew,

One year, absolutely unbelievable. I remember sitting in the aftermath wondering, *What will life look like a year from now?* And today here we are. Somehow one day at a time has added up to 365 days, days of sorrow and joy, days of hope and defeat, days of beauty and pain.

Grief has threatened to steal away everything, but we are still standing, still living, still fighting. Fighting for joy, fighting for beauty, fighting for peace, fighting for life! The fight has taken everything I have every single day. I'm exhausted, but still showing up, still saying yes, and still leading our boys through today and into tomorrow.

As I was thinking about the one-year anniversary, I couldn't get over an Instagram picture you posted. It was a beautiful shot looking out over the lush Hawaiian landscape with light beaming down through the clouds. You captioned it, "In Kauai as it is in heaven." I had to come see what you saw that day, so the boys and I hopped on an airplane and came here, your spot, your heaven, your favorite place in the world.

It hurts so deeply you aren't here with us; I wish I could hold you, kiss you, see your smile, and hear your laugh. I wish you could play with your boys again; I wish you could see how much they've grown. Smith looks like a teenager, Jethro still looks like you just taller, and Brave still thinks he's a baby and asks me to carry him everywhere we go, but his legs are growing long and his vocabulary is growing wide. We are slowly rebuilding a new life; I call it rebuilding beautiful. It's a very different kind of beautiful, and right now it's pretty ugly, but I am choosing to believe one day beauty will surround it.

This trip has been so special. We rented a bright red Jeep, something I thought you would love, and with our windows down, Jack Johnson blaring through the speakers, and the sweet island breeze flying through our hair, we have remembered you. Even though you aren't here, I can't help but see you all over this place. This place holds so many precious memories for you. The times you came here with your family growing up, the special time we spent on our honeymoon here, and the last trip we made with our whole family just a few years ago. This spot has been a healing place for a long time, and even now, it's healing our hearts. It's funny how people look at me when I'm out and about with our boys. I can see them looking for you, I can see their wheels turning, wondering, *Is she really here all alone?* Truth is, I know I'm not alone, I know the veil is thin. I know heaven isn't far but near, I know our time on this spinning ball of dirt is just a pit stop, just a resting place on our way to you, to heaven, to a place even more beautiful than Kauai.

God has been so good to us this year. He has provided above and beyond in every single area of our lives. I set this verse as the background on my phone, and for months it has reminded me to pin my hope in Him: "God can do anything, you know—far more than you could ever imagine or guess or request in your wildest dreams! He does it not by pushing us around but by working within us, his Spirit deeply and gently within us" (Eph. 3:20 THE MESSAGE). He has done great things in and through our pain this year:

He has provided a beautiful bungalow for our little tribe.

He has given me deep purpose in the pain.

He has opened doors for our story to be told.

He has saved countless lives through your death.

He has surrounded us with support and love.

He has provided financially.

He has gifted us beautiful experiences all around the world.

And He has shown us He's got this over and over again.

Andrew, I miss you so much, but I know I will see you soon. This year flew by, and I know every year will be the same. Until then, I will cling to those three little words that have carried us through so much, *God's got this,* because He truly does. He is in every single detail, He is still holding us so delicately, and He is picking up the pieces and putting us back together, one day at a time.

I love you, Drew. I will never stop loving you.

Your Girl[1]

God's got this—three words that entered our world in a small, dark room in the ICU unit of the hospital where my father-in-law, Dave, broke the news of his diagnosis to our family. He said, "The doctors just told me I have leukemia. And there is a kind you want and there is a kind you don't want, and I have the kind you don't want. But God's got this." A significant moment: a moment that changed our family forever, a moment marked by trust and faith, a moment where we declared together, no matter what the outcome, *God's got this*. We didn't know it then, but those three words would become our lifeline.

We made wristbands, built a website, and spread the news of Dave's diagnosis to our church and our community, all branded with the hope of *God's got this*. As the cancer raged through Dave, we ran to God. We continued to trust him despite our circumstances, and we faithfully shared everything we were learning with anyone who would listen. *God's got this* became a message of hope—not just for our family but for families all around the world. All because of an intimate moment in the ICU and a man who served God well. Dave was the real deal, as real as it gets. Humble and faithful, servant, father, papa, pastor, and friend. He taught us how to love better, live fully, laugh often, and lead through pain. He was deeply admired by thousands of people, and he was Andrew's best friend.

The leukemia journey lasted four years. It was a roller coaster of remission and relapse. As a family we lived in and out of the hospital, never knowing how much time Dave would have left. During his first season of remission, Dave was determined to return to the calling he loved, the calling that was stripped away in an instant that day in the ICU. In August 2012 Dave returned to the stage and, together with Andrew, led our church through a beautiful message series called Lessons from Leukemia.

The first lesson Dave shared was this: "Life is about bringing God glory."[2] As I replayed his message years later in the midst of my own grief and loss, all I could mutter through my tears was a quiet, resounding *yes*. It's all about glory, not our glory but *his*. We exist in a world of personal gain and public platforms, and we forget it's not about us. Life from the very start has been and always will be about God and his glory.

Before man ever existed, before the world was formed, before the stars were set into place, it was God and his glory. When he breathed life into dust and set the earth into motion, it was God and his glory. When sin broke everything glorious and good, it was God who sent down his Son in his glory to save us all. From the beginning to the end it has been and always will be God and his glory. From dust we came, and to dust we will return; we are simply reflections of God's glory for our short time here. And when the time comes to say goodbye, we will enter into his glory forever.

The indescribable glory of God—it's hard to find the words yet we try, using words like *splendor, beauty, holiness, presence,* and *light*. The elusiveness of glory beckons an awe and wonder in us. We all need wonder. When did we lose it along the way? That childlike wonder I see in my boys, I want to bottle it up and carry it with me everywhere I go. Wonder reminds us how small we are and how big God is. Wonder keeps us curious; it keeps us engaged, and it keeps us searching for him and his glory everywhere.

Glory is often tied to the word *honor*. We honor someone or something through an attitude of reverence and respect. Honor requires action; without action honor doesn't exist. When I think about honor I think about tattoos—modern-day honor in the form of permanent ink. We pay tribute to the people we love and the things we ascribe value to through painfully marking our bodies forever. I have tattoos: a tattoo that reads "Psalm 139" on my foot; a tattoo proclaiming the names of my sons, Smith, Jethro, and Brave, down the side of my right arm; a cross on the top of my right hand; and two small tattoos in honor of my guy and our story on my left arm, my way of remembering him and honoring him forever.

A few days before Andrew's memorial service, I drove to the small tattoo parlor by the beach, Agape Tattoo. I followed the steps up a narrow stairwell and into a quaint studio space. Peaceful music filled the room, a large, rugged cross was on display, and my friend Kelsey was there patiently waiting for me. It was a sacred moment; Andrew was gone, and I would permanently remind myself of his passing. We were the only ones there, just the two of us and the tattoo artist. I told him my sad story, but he already knew; he had been faithfully praying for our family. The news had found its way to him, and now the sad story had walked into his shop and asked for more pain. Such a small world we live in, but I don't believe in coincidence.

I love how God so delicately orchestrates our lives, how he reminds us of his kindness even in out-of-town tattoo parlors. I explained to the tattoo artist what I wanted, a tattoo for my guy and a tattoo for our story. For Andrew, 2 Kings 22:2, his life verse: "He did what was right in the eyes of the LORD and followed completely the ways of his father David, not turning aside to the right or to the left." A verse he planned to permanently mark on his body, but he never had the chance. And for our story, those three words that had carried us through so much, our lifeline: *God's got this.*

The tattoo artist printed the words on a small piece of paper, and I found the perfect place, on the inside of my left arm just below my elbow. He picked up the tattoo gun, dipped the needle into the thick black ink, and delicately began his work. Andrew sitting in the presence of glory forever and me in a small tattoo shop honoring his name. *How could it be?* A life changed overnight and now a body permanently marked by the change. From the inside out I was transformed. Each etch of the needle painfully reminding me of my humanity, my fragility. I looked in the mirror when he finished and hardly recognized the reflection I saw. Far from a reflection of *glory*, I looked more like a reflection of brokenness, heartache, and pain. So many questions swirled in my mind. *How do I bring God glory here? How do I live as a mirror of his glory in the trenches of pain?*

Life from the very start is a series of mountaintops and valleys. But somehow we are to carry a mirror with us through it all; we are to reflect God in the dark depths of the valley just as we reflect him in the bright light of the mountaintop. But how? How do we cling to *God's got this* and honor his name when life is dark and lonely?

There is a verse and a message illustration that helps with the how. During week two of the Lessons from Leukemia series, Andrew took the stage. He was twenty-four years old but called, equipped, and confident in his plaid button-down shirt and skinny jeans. He took a dry-erase marker in his right hand and carefully drew a horizontal line on a large whiteboard. It wasn't a straight line; instead it started on the far-left corner with a small incline curved up, then drastically declined down and inclined up again on a curve to an even greater height. He called the illustration the Dip. The start of the line marked the place where we accept Jesus for the first time. The lowest point following the harsh decline marked the place where our faith is tested, and the end of the line, the highest point on the board, marked the place where God wants to take us. The illustration looked like this:

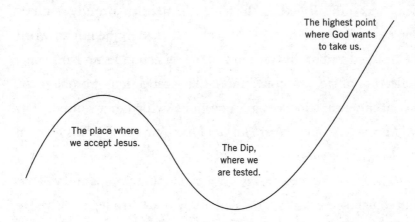

The highest point where God wants to take us.

The place where we accept Jesus.

The Dip, where we are tested.

After Andrew explained the illustration, he carefully picked up the marker again and followed the line one more time. But this time as he followed the line, he read a familiar passage from the book of James: "Consider it pure joy, my brothers and sisters, whenever you face trials of many kinds, because you know that the testing of your faith produces perseverance. Let perseverance finish its work so that you may be mature and complete, not lacking anything" (James 1:2–4).[3] The verse fit The Dip perfectly, and I am so thankful for this beautiful illustration of walking with God through it all. If we hold on to our faith and remember God's got this—through every trial, every wilderness season, and every dark valley in this life—we will develop perseverance.

Perseverance sounds like a good word, doesn't it? Just persevere, just push through, just keep moving forward, and you will be okay. Perseverance is anything but easy; instead it's painfully developed over time. In another translation, the word *perseverance* is replaced with the word *endurance* (NLT), which means the measure of our stamina. Endurance asks the question: How long can we keep going without giving up? It's a word that reminds me of a 13.1-mile journey, my first half marathon through the hills of Seattle. Andrew and I moved to Seattle just a few months after we were married. It was a short but significant period of time, newlyweds off on our own adventure together far away from home. He accepted a position as a high school pastor at a church surrounded by dense, green trees, and I was planning to pick up a few odd jobs as I finished my bachelor's degree.

Two naïve California natives looking forward to living in thick sweaters, sitting by the fire, and being swept away by the sound of rain. We drove up the coast in our small, clunky U-Haul with high hopes and expectations. Upon arrival we were greeted with freezing cold weather and snow and forced to quickly adapt to our new surroundings and learn the ways of the Northwest. What we learned right away was that although the rain was relentless, it didn't stop people from spending time outside. We were surprised to see people running, biking, and walking through the rain and the snow. In hopes of making new friends and adapting to the culture, I signed up for my first half marathon. I would slip into my thick leggings, throw on my windbreaker, lace up my shoes, and head across the street to the park, building up my endurance one run at a time.

It may have been the season we moved, but we literally never saw the sun. The cloud cover was so thick that the sky would become completely dark in the early afternoon. As the newness of Seattle wore off, the gloomy days began to wear us out. We dreamed of sunny California beaches and lying by the pool in the backyard. Just as we began to plan our move back home, we woke up one day and there it was: the sun was shining, the sky was blue, and our world was transformed. We emerged from our small apartment to discover a new season unfolding right before our eyes. New sights, new sounds, and new scenery surrounded us from every angle. We spent the entire day outside reaping the harvest of a long, patient winter. A crystal clear day in Seattle is so extraordinarily beautiful it will take your breath away. The beauty that is hidden in the darkness finally emerges in the light.

It's like our wilderness seasons, isn't it? It's hard to see the light when the rain just won't let up. It's hard to feel the sunshine through the clouds. But without the rain, Seattle would lose its beauty. It's because of the rain that the landscape develops such deep and vibrant colors. Couldn't we say the same thing about our own life?

Our own seasons? If all we knew were sunny days, we would never appreciate their beauty. It is the long, bleak winter that stirs in us a newfound appreciation for the sun. The One who set us here today, for such a time as this, is waiting for us in tomorrow. "All the tomorrows of our life have to pass through him before they can get to us."[4] We can choose to persevere, to press on, to embrace the hard, ugly, and uncomfortable knowing the finish line is waiting for us just around the corner. We can choose not only to embrace today but to endure the elements along the way. When we show up in the seasons where it would be easier to sit on the sidelines, we build the endurance we need to survive the marathon of life.

The Wilderness

Before we moved back to California, I once again slipped on my leggings, threw on my windbreaker, laced up my shoes, and showed up for the race. A 13.1-mile journey over rolling hills, through the woods, in the rain, and all the way into the city. The race was beautiful, painful, and challenging. As I passed each mile marker and grew closer and closer to the finish line, I knew the pain would be worth the glory; I just had to persevere. As I hit the final stretch, crowds of people began to gather around the sidelines. They were holding warm cups of coffee, sitting on cozy blankets. Some were holding signs, others were capturing the moment on cameras, but everyone was cheering and clapping for their loved ones. Finally, I rounded the corner, and there it was: towering high above the crowd, I saw the finish line. As I crossed over the line, I crumbled into tears. I couldn't believe I did it. I couldn't believe I'd endured all of the pain, and I couldn't believe it was over. I pushed my way through the crowd and found my Andrew. He was waiting for me there with a big smile on his face. I fell into his strong arms as he held me close and whispered in my ear, "Good job, babe. I'm so proud of you. Look how far you've come."

When I look ahead at my life, when I think about the finish line that's waiting for me off in the distance, I imagine, just like that day in Seattle, my Andrew is patiently waiting for me there. He is standing on the sidelines cheering me on. As I pass each new mile marker, as I push through the dark valleys of pain, as I dig deep for strength to persevere, I know each breath, each moment, each day is one day closer to glory forever. And I can't wait to cross the finish line, lock eyes with my guy, fall into his strong arms, and hear those same words from his lips. *Good job, babe. I'm so proud of you. Look how far you've come.*

Afterword

Moments

It's been a year and nine months since Andrew died. Six hundred and nineteen days to be exact. During the first year, every day felt like a marathon. Life, it seemed, was only something to get through so that I could be closer to Andrew. In that year I was counting down the days until my death. I wanted nothing more than to enter into eternity with my guy. I didn't want to live without him, and I wasn't sure how I ever would. But I have.

Today, on day 619, I can honestly say I've stopped dreading my days—I've started living them. I've stopped seeing my days as one long road leading me to Andrew, and instead, I've chosen to embrace, to wake up, to grab hold of this one life and live it. During that first year there were reminders of Andrew everywhere, strings tied to him, and with every move I became tangled up in them. But now as I look around my house, the tangled web of grief has slowly withered away, and I find myself sitting in this new life I have made. Every choice, every step, every brave yes that first year—and these last nine months—has led me here. And you know what? I am starting to find comfort. Here is starting to feel like home. I can live in my skin again. There are still strings to Andrew, tied to my former life, but I've learned to live with those too. They have been woven into the fabric of my being, my soul, my story, my home, and my life. The bleak black-and-white world of grief has slowly faded away, and I am starting to see color again. And because I have tasted death, the colors are even more vibrant and beautiful than before.

Here in this new, colorful world I have been thinking about the power of a moment. Life is a series of moments. Most of them are mundane and unseen. They pass us by, and we don't try to catch them. Many are hard and uncomfortable. But then there are rare, captivating moments when time stands still and heaven touches earth, when we are swept away by perfect love, wonder, and awe.

I had one of these moments a few weeks ago—a moment I will not soon forget. Everything leading up to it was busy and hard. The boys and I had decided to camp out in a tent in the backyard. There was setting up the tent, cooking dinner, cleaning up dinner, catching mosquitos that made their way into our tent, and convincing three little boys to fall asleep before midnight. But then at 5:57 a.m., as the sun began to rise and the birds were chirping in the trees, while my three wild boys were still fast asleep, I caught the moment. The one that made all the other hard ones worth it.

I captured it on video: My three beautiful boys still fast asleep. Our little dog, Juno, nestled into the sleeping bag beside Smith. Brave, with his special green blanket draped over his sweet little head to keep his ears warm, only his precious little eyes and nose emerging from the comfy covering. Jet, calm and serene nestled in between the others. I wanted nothing more than to soak it in, to sit still in the moment and allow the love, the wonder, and the awe to completely wash over me. I was swept away; it was magical.

But the thing about moments is, they never last. They are here, and then they are gone. They will never happen exactly the same way again. Our job is just to notice them. To truly catch and hold onto every special, heaven-sent moment as tightly as we can. And to allow them to carry us through all the mundane and hard parts of this life.

I have had some ugly, horrific moments. But I have also had wonderful, beautiful, breathtaking moments. Loss has opened my eyes to see everything differently, and with these new eyes, I don't want to miss a thing. Life—even after loss—is worth living, worth fighting for, and worth rebuilding over and over again. Keep going, friend. Keep catching the magical moments. We are in this together. You are not alone.

Acknowledgments

It was a kind and surprising Instagram message from Lysa TerKeurst, just a month after Andrew died, that set this book into motion, "You are a beautiful writer. In time, if you ever think of writing a book, I'd love to help." I cried happy tears, called a friend, cried some more, and knew deep in my heart that Lysa's message only confirmed the message God was already whispering in my ear: the time for this book was now.

Thank you, Lysa, for the way you have walked alongside me and encouraged these words from the very beginning. The time I spent learning from you and your team at She Speaks really kick-started this whole process. The way you encourage people like me to find the words and pen them down is unparalleled. I am so grateful to call you my friend.

To Lisa Bevere, thank you for continuously speaking truth and healing over my life. Our first conversation about this book was another huge confirmation from God that these words needed to be written. Thank you for opening the door for me to connect with the incredible team at the Fedd Agency.

To my wonderful agent Whitney Gossett, thank you for believing in me and this message from day one. You have been a constant voice of encouragement and I am so grateful.

To my editor Jenny Baumgartner and the team at Thomas Nelson, thank you for taking a chance on me and this story. Thank you for being willing to be brave with me, with this topic, with this message.

To Rachel Hanlon, I am so thankful for your friendship and your unending help with the boys. You created time and space for me to get away and write these words down. You have been a consistent lifeline of support, and I'm pretty sure the boys love you more than me.

To Kelsey Kappauf and Tasha Van Winkle, you are treasured friends. Thank you for faithfully reading every messy rough draft. For your helpful and encouraging words along the way, and for sitting with me in the deep pain. For picking up the phone when I called crying, for speaking words of truth every time I doubted myself, and for continuously pointing me back to God when my faith grew tired and weary.

To the Stoecklein family: Carol, Austin, Paige, and Ashley. We have lived these words and this story together. Thank you for loving me and the boys so well as we navigate this new life. I love each of you deeply, and I am so proud of the way we have leaned into God and declared "God's Got This," no matter what.

To my beautiful boys: Smith, Jethro, and Brave. You are my heroes. Your resilience, your joy, and your love have carried me through my darkest days. This book is for you. We will read these words together one day, and I hope they will remind you how much your daddy loved you and how hard he fought to stay. "You are smart, you can do anything you set your mind to, you are going to change the world, and I love you just the way you are."

To my Andrew, when I told you I wanted to write a book all those years ago, you believed in me. You knew one day the words would come, but I know you never imagined this would be the story I would tell. You were one of my greatest teachers. I learned how to lead through pain from you. Can't wait to see you again soon.

Appendix

Rest in the Wilderness

We have walked through some heavy topics in this book. I wanted to offer space to reflect on what we've learned, a reminder that you are not alone in the wilderness. Grab a journal and a pen, or phone a friend, and honestly explore each of these questions. Let's learn and grow together.

Chapter 2: The Uninvited Guest

1. In what areas of your life are you struggling with fear?
2. If you are walking through a wilderness season, what does it feel like?
3. How have you met with God in the wilderness?

Chapter 3: How Did We End Up Here?

1. How can you trust God in your wilderness?
2. Are you getting the support you need in your wilderness season? If not, in what ways can you reach out for help? Is there a community nearby you can plug into?
3. Is there someone you know who is walking through a painful season, someone who you could personally reach out to and encourage? What would you say to that person?

Chapter 4: To the Back of the Cave

1. When did you last spend time alone? Was it in solitude or isolation?
2. If you are feeling isolated, what can you do to break free?
3. How can you carve out time for solitude?

Chapter 5: Stranger Things

1. Have you experienced spiritual warfare? What did it feel like?
2. Who are three people you could call to pray for you when you are feeling oppressed by the Enemy?

Chapter 6: Hot Mess

1. How has this chapter changed the way you view suicide?
2. How can you support and love those around you who are suffering from the crippling effects of mental illness?

Chapter 7: Goodbye to Everything

1. How have you invited God into your pain?
2. In what ways can you see that God still has good plans for you—even in your mess?
3. What is God trying to do in you while you are in your mess?

Chapter 8: One Plot or Two

1. How has walking through grief or pain changed your relationship with God?
2. In what ways is fear ruling your life?
3. How can you replace fear with hope?

Chapter 9: New Wine

1. What have you learned through your season of waiting?
2. In what place do you feel the most connected to God?

3. Have you experienced a miracle on the other side of your wilderness?

Chapter 10: Rebuilding Beautiful

1. If you could write a letter to yourself, what would you say?
2. What big dream do you have for your life? How can you chase after it?
3. What does your "cup" of suffering look like? What does it feel like? How might you, like Jesus, move toward accepting the cup?

Chapter 11: God's Got This

1. What does perseverance mean to you?
2. How can you reflect God's glory in the valley season?
3. Who do you hope is waiting for you at the finish line?

Find Hope

Helplines

- **National Suicide Prevention Lifeline** is available 24-7 across the United States for those who are worried about a friend or loved one, or who would like emotional support. Visit www .suicidepreventionlifeline.org or call 1 (800) 273-TALK (8255).
- **Crisis Text Line** serves anyone, in any type of crisis. That doesn't just mean suicide. It's a resource for any painful emotion for which you need support. The program provides free, 24-7 support and information via a medium people already use and trust: text. A trained crisis counselor receives the text and responds quickly. Visit www.crisistextline.org or text HOME to 741-741.
- **The Trevor Project** is a national organization that provides crisis intervention and suicide prevention services to lesbian, gay, bisexual, transgender, queer, and questioning (LGBTQ)

young people under twenty-five. Visit www.trevorproject.org or call 1 (866) 488-7386.

- **Veterans Crisis Line** provides confidential help for veterans and their families. The caring, qualified responders are specially trained and experienced in helping veterans of all ages and circumstances. Visit www.veternscrisisline.net or call 1 (800) 273-8255.

Counseling and Treatment

- **American Association for Marriage and Family Therapy** is a great place to start locating a marriage and family therapist in your area. Visit www.therapistlocater.net.
- **American Psychological Association** offers a psychologist locator to make it easy to find a psychologist in your area. Visit www.locator.apa.org.
- **Onsite Workshops** is located on a 250-acre campus in the rolling hills just outside of Nashville, Tennessee, and it has curated transformational emotional-health experiences for the past forty years. Partnering with the best therapeutic and clinical minds in the country, Onsite works to connect the world through empathy, self-awareness, resiliency, and compassion. Visit www.onsiteworkshops.com.

Additional Resources

- **American Foundation for Suicide Prevention** is a health organization that gives community to those affected by suicide and empowers them to research, educate, and advocate against this leading cause of death. Visit www.afsp.org.
- **National Alliance of Mental Illness** is the nation's largest mental health organization and is dedicated to improving the quality of life for people with mental illness and their families through support, education, and advocacy. Visit www.nami.org.

Notes

CHAPTER 1: THE STORY BEFORE THE STORY

1. "Mental Health by the Numbers," National Alliance on Mental Illness, https://www.nami.org/learn-more/mental-health-by-the-numbers.

CHAPTER 2: THE UNINVITED GUEST

1. "Panic Disorder: When Fear Overwhelms," National Institute of Mental Health, 2016, https://www.nimh.nih.gov/health/publications/panic -disorder-when-fear-overwhelms/index.shtml.
2. Mayo Clinic Staff, "Panic Attacks and Panic Disorder," Mayo Clinic, May 4, 2018, https://www.mayoclinic.org/diseases-conditions/panic -attacks/symptoms-causes/syc-20376021.
3. Wayne Cordeiro, *Leading on Empty: Refilling your Tank and Renewing Your Passion* (Bloomington, MN: Bethany House Publishers, 2009), 32–33.
4. Craig L. Blomberg, *The New American Commentary: An Exegetical and Theological Exposition of Holy Scripture*, vol. 22, *Matthew* (Nashville: B&H Publishing, 1992), 159.

CHAPTER 3: HOW DID WE END UP HERE?

1. "Major Depression," National Institute of Mental Health, updated February 2019, https://www.nimh.nih.gov/health/statistics/major -depression.shtml.

2. Carol Stoecklein, "Moving Toward the Mess," part 3 of Hot Mess sermon series (Chino, CA: Inland Hills Church, November 2018), video shared by Inland Hills Church, December 3, 2018, on YouTube, 47:27, https://www.youtube.com/watch?v=SpUfBgW4ZpM.

CHAPTER 4: TO THE BACK OF THE CAVE

1. C. S. Lewis, *Mere Christianity* (New York: Macmillan, 1960), 49–50.
2. Mariana Plata, "When Isolating Yourself Becomes Dangerous," *Psychology Today*, August 29, 2018, https://www.psychologytoday.com /us/blog/the-gen-y-psy/201808/when-isolating-yourself-becomes -dangerous.
3. Julianne Holt-Lunstad, Timothy B. Smith, and J. Bradley Layton, "Social Relationships and Mortality Risk: A Meta-Analytic Review," *PLOS Medicine* 7, no. 7 (July 2010), https://doi.org/10.1371/journal .pmed.1000316.
4. Jane Sandwood, "How Isolation Impacts Mental Health," Mental Health Connecticut, September 1, 2017, http://www.mhconn.org /uncategorized/isolation-impacts-mental-health/.

CHAPTER 5: STRANGER THINGS

1. *Merriam-Webster*, s.v. "edify," https://www.merriam-webster.com /dictionary/edify#note-1.

CHAPTER 6: HOT MESS

1. "Suicide Facts," Suicide Awareness Voices of Education, https://save .org/about-suicide/suicide-facts/.
2. "Suicide," National Institute of Mental Health, updated April 2019, https://www.nimh.nih.gov/health/statistics/suicide.shtml.
3. "Suicide," NIMH.
4. Saint Augustine, *The City of God*, trans. Marcus Dods (New York: Modern Library, 1950), 37.
5. Pope John Paul II et al., *Catechism of the Catholic Church*, 2nd ed., (Rome: Libreria Editrice Vaticana, 1997), https://www.vatican.va /archive/ccc_css/archive/catechism/p3s2c2a5.htm.

6. Shauna H. Springer, "Is Suicide Selfish? Understanding the Suicidal Mind," *Psychology Today*, June 11, 2018, https://www.psychology today.com/us/blog/free-range-psychology/201806/is-suicide-selfish.

7. Edwin S. Shneidman, *Autopsy of a Suicidal Mind* (New York: Oxford University Press, 2004), 8.

CHAPTER 7: GOODBYE TO EVERYTHING

1. Kayla Stoecklein (@kaylasteck), Instagram, August 25, 2018, https://www.instagram.com/p/Bm5B1zWnqWb.

2. Kayla Stoecklein (@kaylasteck), Instagram, August 26, 2018, https://www.instagram.com/p/Bm8wJ6XH397.

3. Kayla Stoecklein, "To My Andrew," *God's Got This* (blog), August 28, 2018, https://www.godsgotthis.com/blog/to-my-andrew-its-only -been-3-days-nothing-can.

4. Andrew Stoecklein, "Mess to Masterpiece," part 2 of Hot Mess sermon series (Chino, CA: Inland Hills Church, August 19, 2018), video shared by Inland Hills Church, August 20, 2018, on YouTube, 57:23, https://www.youtube.com/watch?v=sBWhbn8cMJE.

5. Stoecklein, "Mess to Masterpiece," 57:16.

6. Stoecklein, 58:21.

CHAPTER 8: ONE PLOT OR TWO

1. Kayla Stoecklein, "Mess to Miracle," *God's Got This* (blog), August 31, 2018, https://www.godsgotthis.com/blog/mess-to-miracle-to-my -andrew-today-marks-one.

2. *Merriam-Webster*, s.v. "surrender (*v.*)," https://www.merriam-webster .com/dictionary/surrender.

3. Sue Towey, ed., "Impact of Fear and Anxiety," Taking Charge of Your Health & Wellbeing, University of Minnesota, https://www.taking charge.csh.umn.edu/impact-fear-and-anxiety.

CHAPTER 9: NEW WINE

1. Levi Lusko, *Through the Eyes of a Lion: Facing Impossible Pain, Finding Incredible Power* (Nashville: W Publishing Group, 2015), 24.

2. Kayla Stoecklein, "Wrapped Up in a Cocoon," *God's Got This* (blog), September 4, 2018, https://www.godsgotthis.com/blog/wrapped-up -in-a-cocoon-to-my-andrew-tonight.

3. "Butterfly Life Cycle," Academy of Natural Sciences of Drexel University, https://ansp.org/exhibits/online-exhibits/butterflies /lifecycle/.

4. Andrew Stoecklein, "Grief," part 3 of Endurance sermon series (Chino, CA: Inland Hills Church, October 1, 2017), https://inland hillschurch.com/endurance/grief/.

5. C. S. Lewis, *A Grief Observed* (New York: HarperOne, 1996), 11.

6. John M. Grohol, "Coping with Grief: The Ball & the Box," Psych Central, updated September 11, 2019, https://psychcentral.com/blog /coping-with-grief-the-ball-the-box/.

7. L. B. Cowman, *Streams in the Desert*, rev. ed., ed. Jim Reimann (Nashville: Zondervan, 2008), 439–40.

CHAPTER 10: REBUILDING BEAUTIFUL

1. Kayla Stoecklein, "Six Months," *God's Got This* (blog), February 25, 2019, https://www.godsgotthis.com/blog/2019/2/25/six-months.

CHAPTER 11: GOD'S GOT THIS

1. Kayla Stoecklein, "In Kuai as It Is in Heaven," *God's Got This* (blog), August 25, 2019, https://www.godsgotthis.com/blog/oneyear.

2. Dave Stoecklein, "Lessons from Leukemia: Part 1," sermon (Chino, CA: Inland Hills Church, August 5, 2012), video shared by Inland Hills Church on Vimeo, 57:41, https://vimeo.com/47110358.

3. Andrew Stoecklein, "Lessons from Leukemia: Part 2," sermon (Chino, CA: Inland Hills Church, August 12, 2012), video shared by Inland Hills Church on Vimeo, 43:51, https://vimeo.com/47535954.

4. F. B. Meyer quoted in L. B. Cowman, *Streams in the Desert*, rev. ed., ed. Jim Reimann (Grand Rapids, MI: Zondervan, 2008), 32.

About the Author

Kayla Stoecklein is an advocate for those confronting mental illness. When she isn't busy raising her three young boys, you can find her on the beach, sipping an iced coffee and searching for little glimpses of heaven on earth. Join her on Instagram @kaylasteck and www.kaylastoecklein.com.